THE
OLD
TESTAMENT
IN
THE
CROSS

Only one centurion remained, with a few men,
A very small post to guard that unimportant gallows,
The gallows on which my Son was hanged.

—CHARLES PÉGUY, Night

THE
OLD
TESTAMENT
IN
THE
CROSS

BY J. A. SANDERS

Colgate Rochester Divinity School

HARPER & BROTHERS, PUBLISHERS, NEW YORK

THE OLD TESTAMENT IN THE CROSS

First Edition

B-L

Library of Congress catalog card number: 61-7348

FOR ROBIN DAVID

CONTENTS

PREFACE

History is, as Lord Chesterfield suggested, but a "confused heap of facts," unless and until in it is perceived the sovereign love of God. The terrible and wonderful love of God has manifested itself in history, in Israel and in Christ. In the cross the sovereignty of God, by judgment and grace, reclaimed the world which by the cross rejected it.

What follows is a restatement of what I have been saying in Lenten lecture series in various churches over a five-year period. The folk of Plymouth Church Congregational in Syracuse and their pastor, the Rev. John Huber, particularly insisted I make a book of the series and they must bear some responsibility for giving me the idea to write it all down.

A small gathering of the Federated Theological Faculty of the University of Chicago heard a paper based on parts of Chapters I and II and afforded me the opportunity to rethink and rephrase several points contained in them.

Scripture quotations are generally taken from the Revised Standard Version of the Bible. In a few instances I have used variant readings based on other translations or I have interjected my own rendering of the Hebrew or Greek. I am grateful to the Colgate Rochester Divinity School *Bulletin* for permission to use a portion of Chapter VI which originally appeared in the issue of May 1958, and to Mr. Darrell Lance, a senior at Colgate Rochester, for compiling the indexes.

It is my very real pleasure to express gratitude to three men who read the typescript in the making: Professors George Ernest Wright of the Harvard Divinity School, Samuel Terrien of Union Theological Seminary, New York, and Harmon Robert Holcomb of Colgate Rochester. Their encouragement and their criticisms alike have been most helpful. I alone remain responsible for whatever they feel I should not have said, or, conversely, for the omission of what they feel I have neglected to say.

Rochester, New York   J. A. SANDERS
January, 1961

INTRODUCTION

The cross stands at the heart of the Bible. It is not an isolated event in the biblical story, nor is it a mere historical accident which the New Testament is forced to record. On the contrary, the cross belongs at the center of what the Bible has to say to us.

To the early church the cross was a scandal. Even today most laymen and many ministers are uncomfortable about the cross. Our church calendar unfortunately permits us to observe Palm Sunday, do another week of business, and then the following Sunday join in the joyful celebration of the annual victories of life over death. Omitting the observances of Maundy Thursday and Good Friday, we cancel out any really Christian meaning to Easter. It becomes a pagan festival of some popular fertility cult and we celebrate the resurgence of the sap in the branches and nature's awakening to the call of springtime.

As difficult as the idea of the physical resurrection may be to the critical mind, it is the crucifixion which continues to embarrass 90 per cent of the laity and not a mean percentage of ministers. The resurrection is easily explainable at Easter. It is a beautiful thing adorned with lilies. It somehow proves that God is good to his children. It makes it all right. It is the obviously happy ending that life must have.

Doubts about the resurrection are entertained almost exclusively in seminary classrooms.

The scandal of the cross is the same embarrassment today that it was in the beginning. This does not mean that views of the resurrection which Christians hold or accept are biblically oriented. In truth, they usually are not. But belief in the resurrection is more easily acceptable to the average layman than belief that the crucifixion has anything to say of the judgment and love of God. Churches are packed on Easter Sunday with the joy and exuberance of people everywhere in the beauties and blessings of creation. They come wanting to hear that the upsurging of irresistible hope they involuntarily feel in their hearts at springtime is genuine and God-given and fits into his purposes and plans. By contrast the modern seminary-educated pastor enters his pulpit confused and uncertain. He has worried more about this one sermon than all the rest he has to preach. He is not sure he has anything to say to his people without abandoning his integrity, or using ambiguous phrases about a victory over death about which there is not a shred of evidence from history past or present.

The embarrassment over the resurrection is almost totally limited to the pulpit and the seminary. For the great majority of the laity it is fully acceptable. It is the success story they thrive on. They do not question it for the most part. They do not even think about it. Admittedly it is a nonbiblical and surely unchristian view of it they have, but it is far from being a scandal.

The crucifixion, on the other hand, is a rather uncomfortable thought. How much time, one might wonder, is wasted in church discussion groups and Bible study groups on such questions as Why did God let Jesus die? or How could God let his son suffer so? or on such speculations as If only Pilate had not washed his hands, or Why did not Jesus hide and escape? One of the most frustrating experiences I have ever had came when, after presenting an address on the suffering love of God, a devout, faithful layman put the question, "How can a good God permit such suffering?"

It is something of a shock to realize that at the center of the church, in the chancel and on the altar, stands a symbol of shame, ignominy, disgrace, and injustice. Popular theology whether of the uncritical lay mind or of the "positive thinker" finds such an association with the cross offensive, a scandal. At the heart of the Christian faith is the cross, a reminder of a case of injustice, an innocent man accused, a miscarriage of justice. The cross, not being a hangman's noose, or a sword, or even a modern revolver, has no obvious connection with violence and death. It stands in our Protestant chancels gold plated and pretty, and for the most part devoid of meaning. For centuries Christians have self-righteously wondered how the Jews who sought Jesus' death and the Romans who killed him could have been so cruel and mean and stupid. The cross is such a scandal to them they actually reject it when its historical meaning is understood. For to blame the Jews or the Romans for the crucifixion is to reject the cross. Not permitting themselves to hate the Jews or angrily speculate about what they would have done had they been Pilate, modern churchmen accept the only comfortable alternative—they think positively about Easter and the resurrection, which, they assure themselves, at least means everything turns out well in the end.

The purpose of this study is to induce those who are willing to think radically about the cross, to consider its central place in the church, in the gospel, and in the Bible. The cross speaks harsh, cruel words to a world which has done its best to rob it of its essential power—just as that same world tried to do when it first used the cross to kill the Christ who hung upon it. Harsh and cruel, because that is what the gospel must be before it heals and comforts. The message of the Christian Bible first strips us bare and then it comforts; or rather, it strips us in order to comfort us.

The Bible is a shocking thing, just as the cross is a scandal. Those who read it devotionally, expecting it to give them a "lift," probably don't read much of it until they are forced to permit it to do its deed—strange its deed and alien its work (Isa. 28:21). The cross demands to shock and offend before it soothes and heals. It smites in order to heal (Hos. 6:1); it wounds in order to bind up (Jer. 30:12-17).

The meaning of the cross can be viewed only from the perspective of the whole Bible. To study the cross or the gospel only in the New Testament is like studying twentieth-century man without taking account of all the centuries of man that have gone into his make-up. But the case is stronger than the analogy, for the New Testament itself insists that its rootage is the Old Testament. However, this is not to say that the cross of Christ is in the Old Testament, in the sense that it has often been contended: to do so would permit us to say that his resurrection is in the Old Testament as well.[1] This would then rob the New Testament Christology of any distinctiveness and significance historically and our only honest course would be to have done with it. Rather we must assert that Christ and his cross are in the New Testament and not the Old, but that without the

Old Testament the cross would, as it were, hang suspended in mid-air, inaccessible and irrelevant.

In the modern missionary movement, there was an unsuccessful attempt some decades ago to substitute the literature of local peoples for the Old Testament. The New Testament is rendered somehow shallow and even void by such an uprooting. The Old Testament is the only criterion the New recognizes to test its claims for Christ and the church. The Old Testament is canon to the New. Not only so, it is often the explanation of the New. A case in point, indeed the case in point, is the scandal of the cross. Without the Old Testament the cross remains an offense and has no solid bridge on which to relate judgment to redemption, to perceive that in God's judgment, his sovereignty, is salvation and redemption. The Old Testament literally saves the New Testament as is demonstrated in church history; it saves it from mysticism; it saves it from naturalism; it saves it from gnosticism; it saves it from docetism; and it finally saves it from our shaping it into whatever happens to be our favorite philosophy as the generations come and go—Platonism, Aristotelianism, Rationalism, Existentialism, etc. The New Testament writers felt that what they were convinced of in Christ was firmly rooted in the word of God as they then knew it in the law and prophets and psalms. Their arguments, their presuppositions, and their faith lay grounded in God's revelation to, and covenant with, Israel. For them there was no other foundation, no other criterion, no other canon by which to know the nature of Christ and his church.

Without the Old Testament the cross is an embarrassment if not a sad mistake, one of man's little errors which God fortunately overcame. With the Old Testament, however, the offense of the cross is the judgment of God upon the

world, and at one and the same time his salvation and redemption of the world.

And so we say, not the cross in the Old Testament, but,
the Old Testament in the cross.

THE
OLD
TESTAMENT
IN
THE
CROSS

CHAPTER I

THE CHRISTIAN STORY

The Christian story is a story Christians tell about what God has done in specific moments of history. The episodes which make up the story are recorded in the Bible and in the church. For Protestants, as opposed to Roman Catholics, only the biblical story is canonical or authoritative. Protestants do not deny that God has been active since the first century; on the contrary, they affirm his sovereignty and providence in the church through the ages. Nonetheless, only the Bible clearly contains the victory and power of the word of God through and in and by the word of man. In the church his word and will are understood and discerned through the canonical perspective of the Bible. The church is the locus, not only of the telling and the hearing of the story (the word rightly expounded and rightly received), but in a much deeper sense of the reliving of the story (the sacraments rightly administered and rightly received).

The church's mission and charge as instituted by its Lord is to tell and retell the story, as well as to witness to its truth and power, by services of worship and praise and by reflecting in itself for the world the image of its Lord, the suffering servant. Any understanding of the church apart from that image, the *imago Christi*, is a false one. It is an image bestowed and imprinted upon the church by its Lord who is himself an integral part of the church, its Head. To try to describe the church sociologically is commendable and helpful; but to try to define it by sociological means alone is fallacious. The church is the *corpus Christi* and bears in the world the *imago Christi*—in the same sense that Genesis tells us man bears the *imago dei*. Just as man may not act like it, so the church may not act like it. But the concepts are definitive, in biblical terms.

Improbable in the extreme, the story insists that God has given a final and ultimate meaning to history, the story of man, by his own instrusion into that history. The church testifies to God's providence, the Creator's ongoing work in and of creation. It is the church's strange, very odd tale, this good news that He who created the world is concerned about it and loves it. Odd, because we can neither prove it nor disprove it, this persistent concern and love of the Creator. Nor can we arrive at the plot or outline of the story by inductive reasoning or scientific investigation.

If we were able to gather all the facts of the world together in one place we still would not read in them the Christian story.[1] This is the negative aspect of what is meant by the Christian use of the word "revelation." Dietrich Bonhoeffer has said, "It just isn't true to say that Christianity alone has the answers. In fact the Christian answers are no more conclusive or compelling than any of the others. Once more, God cannot be used as a stop-gap. We must not wait until we are at the end of our tether: he must be found at the centre of life: in life, and not only in death; in health and vigour, and not only in suffering; in activity, and not only in sin. The ground for this lies in the revelation of God in Christ. Christ is the centre of life, and in no sense did he come to answer our unsolved problems."[2] To use God as an hypothesis to fill gaps in our ignorance is non-biblical. The Bible insists that we start with God. His transcendence is not somewhere back up the evolutionary scale to explain how things got started in the process. His transcendence is frighteningly close at hand, or "at the centre of life."

The Christian perspective is a given, a revealed, and quite *ineptum*, as in Tertullian's famous phrase. That is not to say that it is contrary to reason altogether; far from it. But we must admit that nothing in history demands that we conclude with this story. Nor is any pragmatic argument convincing. The Christian story does not win out over other religious systems on the basis of its workability. The Christian "answers" are, indeed, no more conclusive or compelling than any of the others. We must constantly remind ourselves that nothing in the created order is going to come along to "prove" what the Christian story says about the Creator and what he has done. That comfort we surrender and sacrifice the moment we first utter our *credo*. As we shall see in the next chapter, faith is far more radical a thing than a theorem which can be mathematically proved or even an axiom which can be pragmatically demonstrated. To think that proof can issue from the created order to verify faith is to have no faith. To do so is to attribute to the created order the power to judge the Creator. The Christian knows that he must sacrifice forever the petty pleasure of ever saying, "I told you so."

On the other hand, the Christian accepts upon himself the risk that in his *credo* he may be dead wrong. Thus there is no comfort in thinking that if it cannot be proved, it cannot be disproved. He knows that doubt is an integral part of faith, and that even faith that moves mountains does not make him a god, exempt from the doubts that will plague him. That doubt is an integral part of faith is seen not only in such biblical books as Ecclesiastes and Job, but even in our Lord's pitiful cries in the garden and from the cross. It is a faith of total humility; arrogance has no place in it. To be cocksure is to lack faith altogether. To have this faith is to have the only assurance possible for the Christian.

The Christian story is of the ways of God with men. It tells us how God does things and either the story judges us, that is, ensnares and traps and claims us, or it does not. We do not and cannot judge it tenable and worthy of our allegiance, and then claim it ourselves. Rather, it claims us. This is what the Bible means by election: God elects us, not we him. How he does so is the plot of the story.

The Bible does not present us a series of myths of the lives and loves of heavenly beings. The Bible does not report what goes on in heavenly courts among the gods.[3] What it tells us of God in history can, and often does, bear a date line. It happens in space and time, not in mythical heavenly courts. The genius of Israel in relating its faith to the world was in perceiving God's activity in history. The poetic masterpieces of mythology of other cultures are, in the Bible, for the most part demythicized and historicized.[4] This is not to say that Israel borrowed all she tells of herself; far from it. But whatever she borrowed she related it into her history, which for her was really a story of God's providence and sovereignty in her national life. Such is particularly the case in the Book of Genesis where what is clearly myth or legend in the parallel literature of Israel's neighbors becomes "historical" in the Bible. For the faith of Israel was a faith relevant to the known order of creation, not a mystery discernible only to the imagination. What other peoples relegated to the order of mythical adventures of the gods Israel daringly affirmed for the one single God of all creation. This is not to say that myth is totally obliterated in the Bible; it is not. But Israel was never satisfied with mythology. For Israel God was discernible in the knowable, not a mystery in the unknowable. What Israel affirmed about God was what her own history testified to. Israel recited in the liturgies of her festivals God's activity in definite datable events (Exod. 15:1-18; Josh. 24; Deut. 6:20-24, 26:5-9; I Sam. 12:8; Pss. 105, 106, 135, 136; Neh. 9:6-37).[5] The prophets, in their arguments of the relevancy and necessity of divine judgment under the sovereignty of God, appealed to the history of God's dealings with Israel as a canon against which they should measure their provocation of his judgment (Amos 2:9-11; Mic. 6:4-5; Hos. 9:10, 11:1-4, 12:9-13, 13:4-5; Isa. 5:1-7; Jer. 2:2-8, 7:21-26; Ezek. 20). Their arguments of the nature of salvation and restoration subsequent to judgment were also based squarely on the history of past redemption (Amos 3:1-2; Hos. 2:14-15; Jer. 31:2, 3, 31-34; Isa. 43:1-2, 52:11-12, 54:9-10). What this history did not bear of God's revelation was discounted as unimportant (Isa. 45:15, 55:8-9; Ps. 97:2; Exod. 33:12-23; Job 11:7, chs. 28, 38-41). Secret revelations as in private dreams that could not be interpreted in terms of that history were highly suspect (Jer. 23:25-28, 28:5-9; Deut. 13:1-5, 18:20-22). It was the firm, solid, foundational faith of Israel that God was the sovereign Lord of history and that history offered clear-cut controls on the formulation and understanding of her faith.

We have said two seemingly paradoxical things. We have insisted that facts alone will not inductively lead us to God. No reading of them will render the biblical story of God's activity. Only a thing called revelation can bring the insight needed to a perception of that activity. On the other hand, we rightly note that the story itself offers the controls necessary, controls in history, to a right understanding of God's continuing activity. This is the canonical function of the story which is a "history" that has been given significance and meaning by God's intrusion therein.

The question that always asserts itself at this point is that of how we can perceive in history this peculiar story. The answer is that faith enables us to perceive it. But biblical faith itself arises out of history; history is the vehicle of faith. They are ultimately inseparable, the subjective and the objective. H. Wheeler Robinson said, "Our standard of values is itself derived from the history to which we apply it. . . . On any theory of authority, the only ultimate court of appeal must be God, and if God is active in human history, the evidence of His presence must be in that activity itself, and from it, and so from Him, our ultimate standard of values must always be derived. . . . Is not the greatest and most comprehensive fact of that history that it reveals God, and is He not Himself the ultimate and supreme factor, hidden within the religious experience which created the history and issued in the Christ?"[6]

The Christian is one for whom God is the ultimate and supreme factor of history. He is the factor which gives significance to facts, that is, makes them into a story about his sovereignty in history. It is he who makes this meaning in history known to certain men and people who become witnesses to that sovereignty—not as in a mythical drama, but in history and through nature, in the terrible realities men experience. It does not become a mythical tale that captures the imagination. This sovereignty issues in the hard facts of time and space. The facts themselves are not different from what they are to those who are not his witnesses. They are the same facts for the man of faith as for the secular scientist or secular historian. Indeed, the man of faith can be the objective historian doing the investigating. There is a sense in which he can be more objective than the secular historian. For the Christian is committed to God and nothing less; he certainly is not committed to history. The secular historian, if he is to make sense out of the facts, is committed to find some explanatory pattern in them. As we shall see in the next chapter, being committed to the Creator offers total and absolute freedom to investigate any and everything in creation. Being committed to God means being committed to nothing less or other than God, hence totally free to deal with the order of fact.[7] The Christian is therefore totally released from the fear of finding or not finding evidence for or against some working hypothesis. This is a faith which transcends confidence; it is commitment. Nothing among those facts will either prove or disprove God's intrusion into them. The Christian historian can never, will never, turn to his secular colleague to say, "See, I told you so; there's God." Never. Facts do not point to God. God points to facts. And the Christian, with a freedom born of commitment to God, investigates all the facts he can get his hands on.

In 587 B.C. Nebuchadnezzar roundly defeated Zedekiah's forces in Judah and took the surviving leaders and others into exile. His armies were bigger and better equipped than Judah's. Geographical factors account for this; economic factors account for that, etc. The historian works carefully on all the facts and tries to account for them, as he should, be he Christian or not. He goes the full round of cause and effect. He must. The Christian historian does not hedge anywhere. However, he is ultimately free of all the "isms" with which he deals. For this event of 587 B.C. has been transcended by God's revelation to his prophet Jeremiah, that in and through all the facts making up the event God was saying to his people, and hence ultimately to the world, that the vicious cycle of defeat and victory and victory and defeat, justice and injustice, good and evil, has been transformed by God's breaking through it. This is not another meaningless defeat for a weak nation; this is the judgment of God upon our commitment to anything less than him, to his creation instead of to him.

Nothing in all the facts that make up the event of 587 B.C. will prove that God was judging Israel—or disprove it. And so God remains hidden (Isa. 45:15; Ps. 97:2; Job 11:7). God points to the facts, not the facts to him. In the various accounts of Moses' introduction to Yahweh, God speaks directly to the prophet, making it very clear that God takes the initiative and enters the situation he chooses to claim for himself. Moses' conversation with Yahweh in Exod. 33:12-19 (the Yahwist tradition) indicates that God knows Moses though Moses does not know God; God also knows Israel's plight in Egypt though Israel has never heard of Yahweh. Even Moses is not to see Yahweh's face according to this earliest tradition. Yahweh reveals himself "backwards," as it were: he reveals himself in what he does and will do for his people; he is recognizable in his manner of dealing with his people, in his sovereign rule of justice and mercy, in his dealing with man, not in man's dealing with him, in his coming to man, not in man's coming to him.

According to another tradition Moses' introduction to Yahweh is equally clearly God's initiative (Exod. 3—the Elohist tradition). It is God again who points to the facts. "I have seen the affliction of my people. . . . I know their sufferings and I have come down to deliver them. . . . I have seen the oppression. . . . I will send you. . . . I have observed you . . . and I promise." A third tradition on this same conversation (Exod. 6:2-8—the Priestly tradition) is equally emphatic on God's pointing to the facts. "I have heard the groaning. . . . I will bring you out. . . . I will deliver you. . . . I will redeem you. . . . I will take you for my people. . . . I will bring you into the land. . . . I will give it to you. . . . I am the Lord."

Similarly in the cultic recitals as well as in the prophetic historic memory the same emphasis is made on God's pointing to the facts, his revelation of himself in Israel's history. One such recital is imbedded in a cultic ceremony marking the settlement of the land (Deut. 26:5-9). "The Lord heard our voice and saw our affliction . . . and brought us out of Egypt . . . and brought us into this place and gave us this land."[8] Amos uses the same story of God's activity for Israel in his pronouncement of divine judgment on Israel (Amos 2:9-11). "I destroyed the Amorite . . . I brought you up out of the land of Egypt and led you forty years in the wilderness to possess the land of the Amorite and I raised up some of your sons for prophets." The other prophets use the same story of God's sovereign rule over Israel's history in the same way.[9] This story was Israel's canon of faith; and though Israel had no scripture we see that she had a canonical tradition equal in value to a Bible. The prophets had two sources of authority in their claim to be spokesmen for God: their own nonverifiable (and non-falsifiable) experience of God's word in their call, which we must call an internal authority; and this story of God's sovereign rule in Israel's history, the external authority by which the prophets called the people to judgment.

This little canon of history was always cast in terms of God's being the active and effective factor in Israel's history. And yet when we look carefully at that history, omitting the divine factor, we make a rather startling discovery. It turns out to be something like the following: an oppressed slave people rebel and flee their oppression; they wander about in the desert like nomads for about forty years; they engage in numerous battles in an attempt to seek a non-nomadic settlement and home; and they in stages conquer a land where they eventually establish themselves as an autonomous nation among the nations of the Palestinian region. Actually this is the common history of many peoples. Migrations of peoples is a sizable chapter in the history of mankind. Settlement by conquest is another. For a people to rise from the status of slavery to that of autonomy is equally common. That Israel's migration from Egypt to Canaan had its parallels in the histories of other peoples is recognized by Amos (Amos 9:7), the same prophet who insisted on God's special sovereignty in Israel's history (Amos 3:2). Israel's migration and resettlement (1290-1150 B.C.) took place in a period when most of her neighbors, Sihon, and the peoples of Edom, Moab, Ammon, and Philistia were experiencing a similar history of permanent settlement in the area.

What we come to realize, when we compare Israel's history to that of her neighbors or of most other nations of the world, is that there is nothing unique about it. Noth-

ing in her history demands that we see that God was working in it. No responsible historian would or should say that
Israel's history is explainable only in terms of God's activity
in it. For the most part, the cultic recitals and prophetic
summaries of Israel's history, cited above, rarely mention
what we commonly understand as the miraculous. Some
of the amplified summaries and recitals do interject notes
of the miraculous which at best but testify to Israel's faith
that God was and is the most important factor in the story.
As has been rightly said in regard to this miraculous element, the Bible does not claim that God from time to time
suspended history in Israel's behalf; he rather gave meaning to it. He broke into Israel's history with a purpose and
with a meaning, not with the magician's bag of tricks. He
broke through a common case of oppression and rebellion,
victory and defeat, not to make it unique and irrelevant,
but to render it meaningful and relevant for the world to
behold. The few miracles the Bible mentions in Israel's
history are not intended as wonders in themselves to be
gaped at in awe, but serve the single purpose of telling a
story in which even the uncritical popular mind will perceive the hand of God. But certainly the miraculous will
finally no more point to God than do the verifiable facts
open to archaeological research. Every nation's history has
been told with miraculous overtones. The remarkable thing
in these biblical accounts referred to above is, perhaps in the
light of what the anthropologist would expect, the great
lack of emphasis on the miraculous.

What the responsible historian discovers, after working
on Israel's history with all the tools and finds of archaeology
at his command, is that Israel was in no wise exempt from
the problems and vicissitudes of her neighbors. All the fac-

tors at work in their history were at work in Israel's history, geographical, climatic, political, and economic. Israel had no protective fence to shield her from the experiences her neighbors endured under equal conditions. Israel suffered the same life cycle they did, settlement and dispersion, integration and disintegration, rise and fall, victory and defeat, joy and sorrow, comedy and tragedy. No responsible historian would or should say that the facts in Israel's history point to God, any more than he would or should in any other history. Israel's faith surely transcends whatever of the miraculous there is in the Bible which witnesses to it: the facts do not point to God. What the faith of Israel proclaims is that God points to the facts; he breaks into them and transforms them from the meaninglessness they otherwise share into a story about God's ways with men.

If this much is clear then we are prepared to understand the Christian story as a story about God who works in and through the common, transforming the rugged stuff of human existence into a gospel. A blustering tale told by an idiot signifying nothing becomes a love story with an ultimate, the ultimate meaning of life. This the Bible calls revelation. And the meaning of revelation is what we have seen as God's pointing to facts, to history, his intrusion there to give it meaning. It is, therefore, a story of the sovereignty and providence of God perceptible only to faith, man's capacity to know God, that is, to accept his sovereignty and to live by the perspective it affords.

Let us take samplings of how God works. Suppose God has the holy desire to inform the world, his creation, of his love and concern. He has a message for mankind; we call it "good news." He wants to get the message across, a very simple message that can be put in three words, "I love you."

This is the basic content of the theological considerations we call providence and redemption. As we shall later see, it is a terrible love which judges us and strips us bare; it is not a saccharine sort of divine indulgence. But given the kind of love it is, the message can, with some trepidation, be reduced to the three words, "I love you." Now let us see how God goes about it. He chooses a people for himself to witness to his love and deliver the message, and then finally he comes himself. All that seems reasonable enough. Now let us look at the Bible closely.

God in choosing a people selects Israel, a bunch—not even a proper nation, mind you!—a bunch of slaves building the store cities of the Egyptian Pharaoh toward the end of the fourteenth century B.C. Frankly, the selection is a bit of a disappointment. Forgive the analogy, but suppose you were God and you were choosing a people for the job. Why, of course, you would choose Egypt. So would I. You wouldn't need a team of efficiency experts to help you make the decision. Egypt had the biggest army, the greatest wealth, and the most influence in the world at the time. They could have done the job in no time flat. Pharoah could have issued a royal decree to the effect in all his provinces, and to unconquered lands he could have dispatched his armies with a zeal inspired of a holy mission. It would have been the dark man's burden to the world, to sally forth on a crusade to tell the world of God's love—at sword's point. Pharaoh was in the position to cram the message down the throat of every nation he could reach. Any who refused the message could have been roundly defeated if not exterminated. Pharoah would then have set up his colonial offices the world over to insure that the message was being taught and communicated properly. One's imagination fairly soars in thinking of the possibilities. But if it goes far enough we finally realize that we are thinking in the very terms of what did happen during the crusades of the Middle Ages, and the Inquisition in Spain, and even during the days of Western colonialism in the nineteenth century.

Looking at the Bible once more, we see that here there is no paternalism. God never forces himself upon us, never crams his providence down our throats. So God chose a people who were not a people, just a motley crew of slaves, to carry his message, to bless the world.

They were not saints. They were like the rest of us. When they had fled Pharoah and emerged into the desert they began to experience the hardships of independence. They felt the pangs of insecurity that accompany autonomy. They cast wistful eyes back upon the comforts of slavery, a place to live, three square meals a day, the securities of paternalism. "Would it not be better for us to go back to Egypt?" (Num. 14:3). The books of Exodus and Numbers well describe the weaknesses and frailties of this chosen people, their envies, jealousies, feeble vows, and weak wills. In other words they were quite normal. We marvel at this election, that God had chosen to work through such a people; and yet we know that all their rebelliousness was as normal as our own, understandable and excusable, given the circumstances. Yet God was working through them. To be fair we must say that they were not all weakness. They had their good points, strengths and merits too. Later Israel saw herself well reflected in these accounts of her origins and knew she had not outlived them. Collectively, later Israel was caught up in the story of her past so that the deliverance from Egypt was as real to succeeding generations as to the generation of the Exodus (Exod. 12:21-27; Deut. 6:4-25).

God elected Israel because he set his love upon her, not because Israel was saintly or greatly exceptional (Deut. 7:7-8). But the fact that he chose Israel and not Egypt already gives a hint of how he works, of the ways of God with man. The way of Pharoah was paternalism. God dipped into the midst of paternalism and chose a paternalized slave people. Paternalism, as we shall see, is in direct contrast to God's ways.

Israel settled in Canaan, the promised land. There Israel forgot God, lost the perspective and became faithless. God had to remind his people of the covenant established in the wilderness. How he did so again reveals his ways with men. Continuing the speculation previously indulged in, how would you, if you were God, go about reminding them? A royal decree from the king should do it. Or perhaps an exhortation by an elder statesman would bring them around. Lacking these, certain sanctions or inducements might be offered. And then look at the Bible to see how he did it. It says he chose a country bumpkin, a boor, a shepherd named Amos, to go speak in the royal sanctuary at Bethel, to the nobility and royalty and clergy and military leaders gathered there. If the personnel department of a large corporation were to follow the Bible in its selection of men for jobs the personnel director would, I dare say, be summarily replaced.

Amos knew no one. He had no influence, no power, no pressures to bring to bear, no sanctions to enjoin, no authority of his own. He couldn't threaten or induce. He approached the heads of state and government and society in

Bethel with absolutely no more than he approached his sheep. Amos had the freedom of being totally unable to negotiate. He had no letter of introduction which some government or ecclesiastical agency could investigate. He had nothing, save the word of God to preach. Of that he was convinced, but still he had no proof of it. Proof opens the way to disproof. All he had was the internal certainty of his personal experience and convictions, and the external canon of the story of God's dealings in Israel's history (Amos 2:9-11).

These two samples of the way God works show us quite clearly that God does not cram his message down our throats. It would appear that at best he but suggests his love to draw us to him. There is no coercion, no paternalism. Either his revelation, his intrusion into our lives, grasps us and claims us by our free response, or it does not. They also show us that God works in and through the knowable and the known, the common elements of the common life. He does not startle us just for the effect. We shall later see that his judgments in history are not startling for the sake of being startling. His judgments, too, are expressed within the common, though terrible, experiences of the knowable, that which in man's history is well known.

The story reaches its climax in the same manner. When God wanted fully and completely and totally to reveal his love and concern, he did so in a carpenter's son, a country boor from the sticks of Galilee. Like Amos he had no prestige or station, no pressures for coercion, no sanctions for negotiation. He totally lacked the means to power politics. He was a man among men, of lower station than most. Nor did he ever rise, as the typical American hero, from rags to riches, from a log cabin to the White House, from filching apples to stealing railroads. He spoke, nay more, he lived God's word of judgment upon his people and ultimately upon mankind, but he did so in a life that was the common life of the Galilean carpenter, without a shred of the power the world respects and allows to shape its history. He spoke and he acted like the son of God he was, that is, one who never for a moment of his life ever lived outside the sovereignty of God. He never confused the issue, the central issue of faith; namely, that God was God and all else his kingdom. This life and witness brought upon him the tragic end of a miscarriage of justice.

And so the word of God makes its final statement in this Jesus, whose life, like Israel's history, was nothing spectacular or in itself unique. Jesus, like Israel, was not exempt from the vicious cycle of victory and defeat, comedy and tragedy. He was a man among men as Israel was a nation among nations.

But God was in this Christ working, as he had worked in and through Israel. In this Christ we have the incarnation of God in a man. One would expect then a story quite different. In fact the expectations of the Jews, including the disciples, were not met in Jesus. Messianic anticipation in Judaism took many forms, but there is little evidence that it took the form Jesus gave it in the period before his reshaping of it. His image was not that which we find in the apocalyptic writings of the Son of Man, as in Daniel 7:13 and the Enoch literature. Nor was it that of a political messiah, scion of the line of David. Both of these references are made of Jesus in the New Testament, but they both recede finally before the burning image of the suffering servant which the passion accounts in the Gospels establish as the fullest statement of God's word in creation.

Such was the incarnation, God emptying himself, submitting to our injustice, assuming the plight of an innocent, righteous man. We say God was in Christ reconciling himself to the world. But do we know what we are saying? If so, pride is broken and shattered, for we have in misjudging Christ, misjudged God. And when we realize what we have done, which, as we shall finally see, was normal, understandable, and excusable, we know the fullness of the judgment of God upon us, a judgment of suffering love. The Christian who reads the passion account knows himself as Annas and Caiaphas, Judas and Pilate. He knows they were as normal as he is, and he as normal as they. Their excuses are his excuses. And when he realizes what he has done he knows the terrible, awful, radical love of God, which both judges and claims him. The Christian stands utterly naked before the cross. He brings there no excuse, no deceit, no defense, no sham. He knows the love of God which strips him bare, knocks every prop out from under him, and at the same time, redeems him as he is and cloaks him in the same love that judges him.

That is the Christian story, a story about God and his ways with man. He does not force himself upon us. Those who report the birth of this Christ in the legend of Bethlehem caught the truth of the whole story. The God who had chosen slaves and simple shepherds to be witnesses to his sovereignty, when he fully and completely entered the life of man, chose a cow shed, a barn, a manger in a cave, by which to make his regal birth. The King of kings was born, not in royal purple, but in hay. He never forces himself upon us. "I stand at the door and knock." To heed that knock is to know the radical judgment of his terrible love.

CHAPTER II

CREATION AND THE CREATOR

The first chapter of the Bible establishes the most important thought pattern the Bible offers. It is not at all history in the sense that the event of the Exodus is history, or the defeat of Judah in 587 B.C. or the life, ministry, and crucifixion of Jesus. Neither is it simple mythology in the sense of relating the doings of gods on Mount Olympus. To recognize, as the biblical historian must, that Genesis 1-11 is fraught with overtones of Mesopotamian mythology is not to say that Israel accepted those myths as she learned them from Mesopotamian polytheism. She did not. She adapted them to her faith already established in her early history, her deliverance, wanderings, and settlement, the recitals of which were noted in the last chapter.

That Genesis 1 is not a pure myth can be readily seen by comparing it with the Babylonian creation myth, *Enuma Elish*. What Israel gives us in Genesis 1 is a highly demythicized account of creation. While it is not completely historicized, as other foreign myths reflected in the Bible are, it is certainly anything but pure myth.[1] Neither is it presented as history as Archbishop Ussher of the seventeenth century mistakenly assumed, who confidently thought he could assign a date to the act of creation. Many well-meaning Christians of the nineteenth century were caught up in a frenzied controversy which for uncritical minds is still at issue today. Out of that controversy was born modern Fundamentalism which in its extreme manifestations is undoubtedly one of the most regrettable, not to say heretical, movements in the history of the church. It chose to set the Bible against science rather than accept the two as quite radically different statements in radically different categories of thought. Denying God's sovereignty in the realm of the very freedom Genesis 1 affords man in his scientific search, Fundamentalists maneuvered themselves into the position of limiting God. They felt they were saving God by insisting that Genesis 1 and biology were on equal planes, and they failed to recognize the impossible position into which they had worked themselves. They so insisted on the conflict between Genesis and science, demanding that only one could be right, that hordes of thinking men and women took their argument as valid and forthwith left the church. Fortunately, there was a quiet element in the church which did not lose its head, but with the kind of radical faith the Bible inspires had already been at work studying the Bible critically. With the very freedom faith affords, biblical critics neither dodged nor hedged at a single issue. They knew the truth of Genesis 1 was not to be bartered at the price of folly, a simple alternative to a scientific discovery. These liberal or critical men of faith were the unsung heroes of the day.[2] The oddest and strangest turn of all took place when the rabid Fundamentalists turned their fire on these scholars. The seekers and searchers, the honest minds whose faith was so deep that it never ceased to welcome integrity and honesty wherever it was expressed, have also in recent years come under another kind of fire, the fire of overzealous neo-reformationists and existentialist theologians. And again it would appear that quietness and confidence are the strength of the church. Quietly serving both camps, nay all camps of theologians, liberal and post-liberal, are the critical students of Bible, history, and archaeology wherever honesty and integrity are honored.

Neither pure history nor pure myth, what then is Genesis 1? It becomes increasingly clear that it is a theological apologetic or, if one prefers, evangel in liturgical form. The more one studies Genesis 1 in the light not only of the whole of priestly tradition but indeed of the whole of biblical faith down to and including the Persian period (sixth to fourth centuries B.C.), the more one is convinced that this chapter is totally unconcerned with the "how" and "when" of creation. On the contrary, within its liturgical form it is a zealous argument for monotheism, with satirical overtones.[3]

The statement of the argument is radically put; it reaches to the depths of biblical faith. What Genesis 1 testifies to is the very foundation of biblical faith; it establishes the most important thought pattern the Bible offers. That its concern is not with "how" and "when" is seen in the contradictions contained within Genesis 1 and between it and Genesis 2. For instance, when one asks how God went about creation Genesis 1 offers two clearly distinct answers. The one answer is that of divine fiat, as is seen in the jussive verbs *yehi* (let there be), *yiqqavu* (let . . . be gathered), *tadshe'* (let . . . sprout), etc. The other is that of active divine labor as is seen in the indicative verb *vayya'as* (and he made, 1:7, 16, 25). The verb *bara'* (create, 1:1, 21, 27) seems to cover both notions.[4] The tradition with which the section ends (2:1-3), namely, God's sanctifying the seventh day and resting thereon himself, confirms the second answer, that of divine labor; it ends on the infinitive of the verb which means labor (la'asot).

The priestly school which put this liturgy into its final form before it was written as a part of scripture hereby was stating one of the two legs of early Judaism, Sabbath observance. The other leg, circumcision, is not established until the section on Abraham (Gen. 17:10). But what is said about the Sabbath is by no means the important statement in the priestly account of creation, as we shall see. Nor certainly was the manner of creation the important statement. If it had been we should surely not have the two types of verbs with all they imply used in the liturgy. In other words, two traditions from the early oral forms of the liturgy are preserved in a "harmony" which placed no importance whatever on how God created his creation.[5] (It is highly possible also that the same two earlier traditions are reflected in the two words used in 1:26 meaning "image" and "likeness" [tselem, demut].)

Nor was the priestly school, which had a large hand in the final editing of the Hexateuch, particularly interested in the question "When?" If it was it shows no perturbation whatever over the different sequence of the process of creation seen in Genesis 2 when compared with Genesis 1. The account in the second chapter says that man was created first, while in the first chapter man is created last. Manifestly the chronology of creation is totally unimportant to biblical thinking. The question "When?" does not arise from any serious consideration of what the Bible itself is saying in Genesis 1 and 2.[6]

What we must note then, in frankly and honestly facing up to these contradictions, is that whatever the Bible is trying to state in these chapters it has nothing to do with the method or the chronology of creation.

Some critical students have gone on to assert that the main point of chapter 1 finally does have something paradoxical to say about chronology, that is, Sabbath observance. That the priestly account of creation (1:1-2:4a) seems to reach a climax in speaking of God's resting on the seventh day of creation and sanctifying it cannot be overlooked.[7] But to say that Sabbath observance is the main concern of the priestly account of creation is to miss the real statement it makes and hence to minimize what we shall see as the foundation faith of the Old Testament as a whole. If the main point of Genesis 1-2:3 is Sabbath observance then it is little more than priestly propaganda of the essence of Judaism, a way of life or a ritualistic system centering in keeping the Sabbath. The final edition of the Decalogue in Exodus (20:11) reflects the same priestly insistence on Sabbath observance whereas the final edition of the Decalogue in Deuteronomy (5:12-15) shows no such priestly revision. In the first, Sabbath observance is derived from God's resting on the seventh day at creation; in the second, Sabbath observance is viewed as a commandment deriving from God's revelation in the Exodus. There is no doubt that the priestly group did insist on Sabbath observance as a definitive characteristic of Judaism as seen in Genesis 2:1-3 and Exodus 20:11. Sabbath observance was important to it.

However, as we shall clearly see, the principal statement of Genesis 1-2:4a is by no means so restricted in scope. What it said to those who first knew it and what it says to us is both radical and universal, universal in a sense so broad that little can compare with it. We have called it a theological apologetic, or evangel, in liturgical form, a satirical and zealous argument for monotheism. It is a statement of faith if by the word we mean something other than a treatise on the same plane as a biological or geological paper; faith, if by the word we mean a radical assertion which cannot be arrived at by science inductively; faith, if by the word we mean a "given" in the realm of God's relation to his creation. The modern mind is so conditioned by the humility of the scientist before the evidence that we somehow distrust the word "faith." We much prefer "to get the facts" first and then cautiously arrive at conclusions. As was pointed out in the previous chapter, such an attitude is not only good, it is precisely the freedom that the faith expressed in Genesis 1 offers.

In other words, the faith expressed in Genesis 1 is that which offers freedom to investigate facts. Genesis 1 does not offer facts to be investigated; it offers the freedom to investigate all facts. Genesis 1 does not deal in facts as a biological treatise deals in facts. To think that it does is to make the same mistake the Fundamentalist has made.

What is the faith expressed in this opening chapter of God's word? Far from saying something about facts or debatable hypotheses which attempt to account for facts, it says something about God. What it says reaches to the depths of the biblical perspective. It establishes for biblical thinking its most fundamental thought form.

"In the beginning God created. . . ." That is the thesis of the whole chapter. There are two categories of being, Creator and creation. In the one there is God and God alone. In the other is all else. The one is unique, singular, and exclusive. The other is plural, multiple, and inclusive. The one is God; the other is everything else. Nothing in the one, God, is created. Nothing in the other is God. They are radically distinct, eternally distinct. They are so radically distinct that what may be said of the one cannot be said of the other—save in our feeble efforts to say anything at all about God in which we are driven, as is the Bible, to making analogies and speaking of God anthropomorphically and anthropopathically. God is, however, ultimately free, save where he chooses to limit himself, of all our analogies, indeed of all our theologizing. Unless the theologian finally admits he cannot, does not, limit God even in his finest system of theology he too has missed the point of Genesis 1. The theologian must make forever the awful admission that he may be dead wrong. In other words, the theologian must above all men keep ever before him this radical distinction; if he does not, he blurs the distinction and is in danger of fancying himself to be God. For who knows precisely when or where, for all the Bible reveals of God's ways with men, God of his own will himself has chosen to breach the distinction?

The humbling effect of such a realization comes in attempting to understand biblical faith. For once this radical distinction between Creator and created is established the Bible proceeds forthwith to say that God himself is constantly violating it. But it is a violating, a breaching, never a fusing or a blurring. The distinction is radical not superficial. When God intrudes into his creation he is God, not man or nature; he does not leave off being God. And so the distinction is absolute.

God is the subject of creation; all else is created. The impact of such an assertion in biblical times was upon a thought pattern quite foreign to our own. Genesis 1 presented a thoroughgoing monotheism to a polytheistic age. This is not to say that we moderns are totally emancipated from polytheism; we are not. But our polytheism, our divided allegiances and commitments, are subtle. In the world of the earliest proclamation of Genesis 1 polytheism was patent. It was the norm of the best thinking the world knew as may be seen in the works of the Greeks and the Romans of the first millennium B.C. Closer to home for the Israelite it was the way his neighbors the Babylonians, the Egyptians, and the Persians looked at the world. Israel's normative faith, if the Bible reflects it clearly, was never polytheistic. It had always been monotheistic at best, henotheistic at worst.[8] Genesis 1 spoke unequivocally in the context of polytheism and naturalism for monotheism, and it did so in terms which the ancient Israelite, or for that matter his neighbor, understood clearly.

It has long been recognized that Genesis 1 reflects mythological language. It has been suggested that Genesis borrowed heavily from and was indebted to the Babylonian creation myth, *Enuma Elish*. In fact scholarly debate usually assumes this to be the case and discussions fall around the question of when and how Israel came by such Babylonian wisdom.[9] Critical debates such as these are necessary and must not be belittled. But when it is assumed that Israel is the grateful debtor the point of Genesis 1 again is missed. What we must realize is that Genesis 1 is not accepting what the Babylonian or Egyptian myth wills to it; it is fighting those myths at every turn. It meets them head-on and mercilessly denies any truth to them, and it does so by using the language and often the imagery of its counterparts. Genesis 1 meets the common creation myths of its day on their own ground, so to speak, and using mythical language and its own assertions, proceeds to transform every issue into its radical statement about the Creator and his creation. Seen in this light Genesis 1 is not indebted to the *Enuma Elish* of Babylon or the Egyptian *Book of the Dead;* it poses itself as their antagonist.

Hence we call Genesis 1 an apologetic in liturgical form. It has a *tendenz* motif running throughout from first verse to last (Gen. 2:4a). It is a vigorous claim upon the mind of the Israelite who might ever be seduced to worship the gods of his more powerful and successful neighbors. It meets his thinking where he entertains doubts about the sovereignty of God. And it does so not only in the majestic style of a liturgy which it undoubtedly originally was; it does so in the satirical tones so dominant in early postexilic Jewish writings beginning with Deutero-Isaiah's ridiculing idols, tones that remained in Jewish literature through Roman times and beyond.[10] The suggestion that Genesis 1 is in any sense a satire needs careful consideration.

The basic suggestion here is that while Genesis 1 is fraught with the vocabulary and concepts familiar to the ancient creation myths, it lends no support whatever to those myths; on the contrary, it attacks and denies them at every turn. The major thesis of the chapter is that there are two radically distinct categories of being, that of Creator and that of creation. Pursuing that thesis the whole account denies any validity whatever to the "theologies" of Israel's neighbors. And it does so in a devastatingly simple development of the major thesis: namely, all that Israel's neighbors call god or gods are no gods at all; they are but of the same order of creation as man himself. Since there is only one God in the one category of Creator and all else is created, it follows very simply that nothing listed in the order of the created is divine, or God. What Genesis 1 then proceeds to do is to list many of the major deities of the religions of Israel's neighbors in such a way that the myths of those religions are brought to mind. Critical scholarship which has seen that Genesis 1 reflects those myths is quite right and must be taken seriously. But it is a reflection which is totally free of any real indebtedness. The manner of creation hinted at in Genesis 1 but serves to bring the polytheistic myths to the reader's mind so that he will recognize that what is here asserted is radically different from what he knows in the myths.

Compare Genesis 1:1-3 to the opening lines of the *Enuma Elish* and note the two things, the similarity and the radical difference:

In the beginning God created the heavens and the earth. The earth was without form and void, and darkness was upon the face of the deep; and the spirit of God was moving over the face of the waters. And God said, "Let there be light"; and there was light.

When on high the heaven had not been named,
    Firm ground below had not been called by name,
Naught but primordial Apsu, their begetter,
    (And) Mummu-Tiamat, she who bore them all,
Their waters commingling as a single body;
    No reed hut had been matted, no marsh land had appeared,
When no gods whatever had been brought into being,
    Uncalled by name, their destinies undetermined—
Then it was that the gods were formed within them.[11]

Heaven and earth are the topic of the opening lines of each. Apsu and Mummu-Tiamat whose waters commingle become *tohu* and *bohu;* "formless" and "void" in the biblical text.[12] "Earth" is a "deep" (*tehom*—compare Mummu-Tiamat) of waters until the firmament of Genesis 1:6 is created in the midst of it. The importance of having a name, which is recognized in the *Enuma Elish*, is equally emphasized in Genesis when God names each item in creation.[13] Such comparisons and parallels have been duly noted and worked and reworked; they are listed and dealt with in the responsible commentaries on Genesis.[14]

The differences, however, are of greater importance, for they shed the light necessary for interpreting the similarities. In Genesis God is not formed or created in the sense that the Babylonian gods were said to be formed. In Genesis there is God and then there is his creation. God is not created; he is Creator. All else is created. This is *the* radical difference. The tone for Genesis 1 is now set. How utterly absurd that any Israelite, or Jew, or anyone for that matter, should worship these so-called gods which are not gods at all! They are but a part of creation the same as man. They are of the same order of the created as man is.

This is the basic statement of the biblical account of creation. The rest of the chapter follows apace, relentlessly relegating every god Israel had ever learned of from her neighbors to the order of creation. Israel knew of the idea of the world egg over which brooded a spirit, as a bird, giving birth to creation.[15] Genesis 1:2 says the spirit of God hovered. Theological speculation over why the word "spirit" is introduced here, which is foreign to the rest of the chapter, is meaningless unless it recognizes that what the writers wanted to do was to call to mind the picture of the egg myth in order to deny it altogether. This is God the Creator who is creating his creation. Any importance the Israelite attached to the egg myth forthwith vanishes. This is a statement about the one God who alone is God; thoughts of brooding birds or spirits have no place here.

And then light is created and it is separated from darkness. These are not the gods of light and darkness, Ahura-Mazda and Ahriman, as the Persians believe; they too are but a part of creation, the same as everything else, the same as man (cf. Isa. 45:7). How utterly absurd to worship the gods the Persians worship! They are not gods at all.

Genesis 1 moves apace cutting like a sword through the categories of gods the Israelite has heard of and whom he has been tempted to worship, ridiculing any notion of thinking them gods at all. The sun god Shamash, Hammu, or Re, or by whatever name he went among Israel's neighbors, is shown to be but another item in the created order. So the moon god Sin and the various star deities. Genesis 1 moves through its simple yet devastating argument with the same depth of conviction Deutero-Isaiah had in his satirical treatment of idols (Isa. 40:18-20, 41:6-7, 21-29, 44:9-20, 46:1-7; cf. 51:9-10).

Perhaps the most telling blow is dealt the Canaanite fertility god Baal, or any fertility god, in the verses on the creation of vegetation and animals (Gen. 1:11, 12, 20-25), for here not only are the vegetable and animal kingdoms brought into being but the process of regeneration itself is a part of creation. In the case of vegetation each category bears its own seed of reproduction, and in the case of animals, *as well as man*, the very first commandment God gives is "Be fruitful and multiply." The very essence of the Canaanite fertility cult is undercut, for fertility is here seen as an integral part of creation itself. How utterly absurd, then, that Israel or any people should worship fertility! That too is but a part of the created order and certainly not a god. Here is the same depth of conviction seen in Hosea's consummate treatment of Baal worship (Hos. 2:2-20 [Hebrew: Hos. 2:4-22]). Sex is an integral part of creation and constitutes the first blessing of God, the commandment to be fruitful and multiply. Old Testament law countenances no perversion of sex nor its excesses (Exod. 22:16-19; Lev. 18:6-23; Deut. 22-23). However, it never condemns sex in its normal expression; on the contrary, it blesses it.

The section on the creation of man carries the argument from God to the worshiper directly. "Let us make man . . ." (Gen. 1:26). It has long been recognized that Genesis here reflects the Babylonian myth which states that Marduk, the principal god of the Babylonian pantheon, took counsel with Ea, a sort of senior deity, before making man with his own blood; hence the expression "Let us make. . . ." Certainly the liturgy is not all of a sudden introducing a polytheism where it everywhere else vigorously denies it. Here, as in Genesis 3:22, we have a reflection of polytheism which calls to mind the myths familiar to the Israelite or early Jew in order to make the contrast with them.[16]

God makes man in his own image. This can only mean what the psalm which mirrors Genesis 1 says it means. God made man lacking but a little of being God (Ps. 8:5 [Hebrew: Ps. 8:6]). Man is created on the sixth day along with other animals (Gen. 1:24 ff.) but he is straightway commanded to have dominion over them, as over the fish of the sea and the birds of the air (1:26). Man is created male and female and forthwith blessed by the commandment to be fruitful, multiply, and to fill the earth and subdue it and to have dominion over all animal and plant life (1:27-30). Man then is charged from creation to be master over the rest of the created order.

Thou hast given him dominion over the works of thy hands, Thou hast put all things under his feet.

[Ps. 8:6 (Hebrew: Ps. 8:7)]

The picture is clear. There are the two orders, that of the Creator, unique and God alone; and that of created, all else, that is, creation in its totality, all nature. However, within the created order man is distinguished by the commandment to have dominion over the rest of creation. That is, he is created in the image of God. God alone is God and hence Lord of all. Man is within creation lord of the rest of creation, by the commandment of God.

How utterly absurd then that man should worship that which he is lord over! How foolish that he should worship some part of that creation, some nature god, sun, moon, stars, fertility, or what not! Israel's neighbors may be more powerful or may have political and economic dominion over Israel, but this does not mean they are worshiping God. The Israelite whose faith was the radical faith of Genesis 1, was never seduced by the attractions of his neighbors to worship their nature gods. He knew they were not gods at all. How ridiculous that man should worship that which he is commanded to be lord over by the one true Creator God! The gods of the Babylonians, Assyrians, Egyptians, and Persians are not gods at all; they are but part of creation like man; nay, they are under man's dominion by order of God.

The section ends with a phrase that sets the tone of the whole. "These are the generations of the heavens and the earth in their createdness" (Gen. 2:4a[17]). It has been rightly observed that there is no theogony (or account of the genealogy or birth of the gods) in the Bible. Yet, in the same sense that we have seen reflections of mythology throughout Genesis 1, so here we have an obvious attempt to call to the Israelite mind such a theogony as he would know it in his neighbors' myths. The word for generations in Hebrew (*toledot*) is from the root meaning "to give birth." In other words, the satire of the whole reaches its climax in the final phrase of the section. In all the solemnity one can imagine, this chapter, which radically and devastatingly denies the existence of any of the gods Israel's neighbors worshiped, ends with what was undoubtedly a phrase common in the Persian or Babylonian rites which the early Jews heard so often—a phrase marking the closing of the recital of the theogony of some great pantheon: "These are the generations of the heavenly and earthly nature deities in their createdness." In other words, they are not gods at all. They are but a part of nature, of the order of the created, and man is commanded to be their master.

The faith to which Genesis 1 testifies is man's creatureliness under God, his Lord, but also man's lordship over nature. It is a faith which is a radical commitment to God and a radical freedom from all else. Committed to God and God only, the man of faith is free to search out and investigate all else. He knows that for all his searching he will not find God, for God is not in the created order; he is Creator. Unlike man he is not trapped in nature. The biblical man of faith knows that God is not to be found in the sun or moon or stars or sea or in any form of nature, no matter how beautiful, no matter how much it may reflect the unsearchable mysteries of man's experiences. Neither the snowflake nor the sunset contains him. One of the non-

biblical notions the Christian finds most difficult to surrender is that of having within himself a spark of the divine,
something inevitably divine in his breast, which somehow
guarantees his personal immortality, or an indivisible measure of mortal goodness. Psalm 8, again reflecting Genesis 1,
states that God made man lacking but a bit of being divine
(Ps. 8:5 [Hebrew: Ps. 8:6]); but nowhere does the Bible
suggest that man harbors within him some divinity. As we
shall later see, the Bible goes much further and says God
has given himself totally to man. But the idea that each
man naturally or inherently closets a pinch of divinity is
totally nonbiblical.[18] We are rather "the people of his pas-
ture and the sheep of his hand" (Ps. 95:7), and he is our
God. The distinction is radical.

This is the basis of biblical faith. Any understanding of
biblical faith is based upon it. Man denies that faith and
abrogates it whenever he does either thing: whenever he
fancies himself to be god; or whenever he accepts anything
else as his god. Man's commitment and allegiance are to God
and God alone but he is master over the rest of creation.
As Paul says, in Romans 6:15-23, the question is who is
slave and who is master. Man is commanded to be master
over the rest of creation, over all God's gifts and blessings,
all the while that he is slave or servant to God. He must be
servant only to God; to serve anything else is to sin. In
other words, whenever man himself attempts to bridge the
distinction between Creator and creation, either by fancying himself divine, crossing the line one way, or accepting
something else in the created order as divine, crossing the
line the other way, he sins.

What then is biblical faith? Defining faith and clarifying
the radical sense of biblical faith are the mandatory tasks of

the church today. Usually in the churches and church schools when an attempt is made to give meaning to the word, it is done by analogies. Words like "faith," "love," or even "music" often defy definition. And so many of the best attempts are done by offering a sense of "what it's like." Undoubtedly every person who ever attended Sunday School knows of such analogies. Faith, we are told, is what you have when you sit in a chair—that it will hold you up and support you. Or, faith is what the mariner at sea has when with his sextant he shoots the North Star to plot his course. Or faith is what the science student has in the laboratory—that, other things being equal, two parts of hydrogen with one of oxygen will yield water. These are things that we do not worry about or have to test every time before using, or basing the future on them. And so we say we have faith.

And yet these are precisely examples of what the Bible says is *not* faith. These are excellent examples of confidence in nature or the created order, in the wood and the workman's skill in the chair, in the North Star's being where it ought to be, and in the constancy of nature and its functions. This is the sort of confidence man must have in order to live out his life. Man puts one foot in front of the other only on the basis of confidence in nature and his fellow man. It is a confidence, however, which is in no sense absolute. It is a confidence man puts in the created order, which indeed he must put in the created order; but it is a confidence based finally on percentages. The chair will someday decay; the North Star is on occasion clouded from view; and it is possible that "other things" are not "equal" in the scientific laboratory. The percentages vary greatly among chairs, weather conditions, and qualities of experiments. They vary greatly among people whom we trust in the day-to-day economy of living.

To have confidence or to put confidence in nature and people is to judge them reliable. The judgment may be conscious or unconscious; it may be a personal judgment or a habit deeply ingrained in the collective subconscious. It has to do with the realm of possibilities and probabilities, the created order toward which man is free to express his confidence or not.

But the man of biblical faith knows this is not what the Bible means by faith. Man does not judge God reliable before he puts his faith in him. He knows that it is God who judges him. And when he knows this he has faith, for faith is not a confidence, it is a commitment, a radical perception that God alone is God, the Creator of all the world who is concerned with what he has created. H. Wheeler Robinson has said, "We often speak of trusting God; is there not often a neglected truth in the thought that God is trusting us?"[19] God judges us and in judging us sustains us for his purposes. We do not in our trusting him (Ps. 4:5 [Hebrew: Ps. 4:6], *et passim*) judge him; we rather accept him as God, Creator, judge, sustainer, and redeemer. The philosopher may speak of God as man's ultimate concern; the Bible speaks of man as the concern of the Ultimate.

In order to deal with the meaning of faith we have gone beyond the simple statement of Genesis 1. But the concern of God for his creation must be seen in the light of the basic categories of faith the Bible's first chapter establishes. To speak only of God's concern for man or of his love for what he has created is misleading. Without the perspective of the radical distinction we have seen between Creator and creature, God's love is misconstrued as whimsy and license.

By the perspective of Genesis 1, basic to the whole Bible, his love and concern are judgment. By that judgment are we sustained and only by it are we redeemed from all our failure to abide by the role which God has set us to fulfill, that of not being God, yet being masters of his creation. To fancy ourselves gods or to fail to be masters we sin, we lose the perspective.

And so this faith is a seeing, a perception, a commitment. It is not merely confession and certainly not an accepting of what we rationally abhor or think foolish. It is a commitment, an active accepting of God's Lordship and sovereignty. It is a "knowing God" (Hos. 4:1, 6:3, 14:5-6; Jer. 5:4-5, 9:3), knowing and fully accepting his lordship and sovereignty. It is knowing that he knows us. It is commitment, finally, to his commitment. God's is the prior commitment. He moves first toward us. He intrudes into our lives, says the Bible, and faith is our knowing, accepting it, our commitment to his commitment, to the concern of the ultimate for his creatures, the love of the Creator for his creation, as well as our obedience to his charge to be servants of his and masters of all else.

CHAPTER III

SIN AND PROVIDENCE

The radical distinction which Genesis 1 establishes between Creator and creation is violated in two ways: by man's sin and by God's providence. Immediately after affirming this absolute and categorical distinction the Bible proceeds to show, on the one hand, how man desires to supplant God in his life, either by giving allegiance to something other than God or by fancying himself to be god; and, on the other hand, how God constantly is breaking through to man. The one is rebellion and the other is revelation; the one is sin and the other is providence, or God's claim of sovereignty over creation.

God did not just create his creation and then abandon it. He did not throw out a finished job to let it make its own way. The Bible asserts that God has from creation been active in his handiwork, constantly meddling and intruding. To say that God constantly violates the distinction is not to say that God leaves off being God any more than to say that man leaves off being man when he sins. What it does mean is that both God and man are in some sense affected. Man in failing to be master of creation, that is, in failing fully to reflect the *imago dei* within the created order, falls short of his appointed place in that order; he fails to fulfill his appointment. God, too, when he stoops to reclaim that appointment for man, in some sense limits himself in his condescension. By his own will he involves himself with man, knows his plight, loves him and finally enters the life of a man, the man we call the Christ.

But neither God nor man, on either hand, leaves off being God, or man. The basic thought pattern established in Genesis 1 obtains throughout the biblical story: God is God and man is man. There is never a simple fusing of the two. The church in its amazing wisdom knew this at the Councils of Nicaea, A.D. 325, and of Chalcedon, A.D. 451, where beyond and through all the theological jargon the nature of Christ was affirmed as fully God and fully man. The faith of the Christian is anchored in the radical distinction of Genesis 1 which is fully confirmed in Christ. Christ was a man, fully, completely, and totally. That in Christ God was reconciling the world unto himself in no wise means that God deprived Christ of being a man. Nor was God any less God for doing his work in Christ. Jesus did not snare or capture God; nor did he deprive God of being God. On the contrary, of all men who ever lived Christ most let God be God by the character and nature of his life. The faith of the Christian is precisely that Christ fulfilled and obeyed the commandment of God in Genesis 1 that man be master and lord over the rest of creation, never failing to distinguish Creator from creation. He let God be God, on the one hand, accepting God only as God; and on the other hand, he never submitted to anything in the created order, never paid allegiance to, or succumbed to, or committed himself to anything less than God. Whatever else the temptation scene of Matthew 4 and Luke 4 has to say, it clearly establishes Christ's refusal to play god himself or to commit himself to aught else than God. Obedience was the content of his life. That he was obedient unto death means the two things: that his life was one of obedience and that his obedience cost him his life.

The content of the biblical story as a whole is made up of the two violations of the Creator-creation distinction of Genesis 1: sin and providence, rebellion and grace; man's idolatry and God's sovereignty. These are the plot of the story. The intensity of the involvement of man in the providence of God bursts into all its fullness in the story of Abram, or Abraham, and Isaac.

An aspect of sin, as the Old Testament presents it, is the failure to choose God. This aspect is perhaps nowhere in the Old Testament more desperately described or more emotionally presented than in Genesis 22, the story of the Sacrifice of Isaac; or as the Rabbis more aptly called it, the Binding of Isaac. I doubt that any other single chapter in the Old Testament, outside Isaiah 53, has so captured the imagination of Christian theologians through the centuries, to convince them of the necessary relation of the Old Testament to the New. But the relevance of the Testaments is not the problem before us at the moment. The reality of sin is nowhere in the Old Testament more grippingly presented than in this short story of a father's love for his son.

The story starts in Genesis 12. There we are told that Abram receives a command from God to leave his country, his kindred, and his home to go to an unknown land. Accompanying the command is the blessing that God will make of Abram a great nation and that he and his descendants will be a blessing to all the families of the earth.

Abram is asked to sever himself from his background, to deny himself all the securities and comforts of his father's house and family, to snip his name from the family tree. In return God would make Abram the patriarch of a great family and nation after him. His children and descendants would be as numerous as the stars of heaven, the sand on the seashore (22:17), and the dust of the earth (13:16).

Such was the command and such the promise. But the familiar chapters that follow relate of one frustration after another. Sarah, his wife, remains barren until she is ninety (17:17) and has "ceased to be after the manner of women" (18:11). At least once Sarah is in danger of being taken as another man's wife and Abram's life is more than once in jeopardy. When all hope is abandoned of Sarah's bearing Abraham even one child, much less a good start on the progeny promised, it is announced that Sarah will bear him a son (17:16, 18:10). Their despair and frustration have been too much and the would-be parents laugh at the idea of having a child so late. Such is the folk-etymology of Isaac's name which means "he laughs." Isaac's name veritably means "joke."

But it was not a joke, for Isaac was born the son of his parents' old age (21:2). And then we come to the story in Genesis 22. It would be difficult to describe the love Abraham had for Isaac, just as difficult as it would be to describe any father's love for his son. But for Abraham it was all the more intense in that Isaac was his only son, the son of his extreme maturity, and most of all, the promise of God.

Isaac was, as it were, the down payment, the earnest show of God of his promise and blessing. Isaac bore the whole of God's blessing that Abraham would become a great nation, a blessing itself. In Isaac was the hope of fulfillment, the depository of blessing. Isaac was in the fullest sense God's blessing, God's gift, the incarnation of a promise.

But Isaac was nonetheless Abraham's beloved son, in whom, we can imagine, Abraham poured all the love a father can pour in a son. And this is the crux of the story in Genesis 22. Verse 2 betrays the fullness of that love and hence the horrible agony in Abraham's breast to learn of this last frustration, the worst of them all. No one should ever read this terrible chapter without reading this second verse again and again and again, before proceeding to the rest.

"Take your son, your only son, Isaac, whom you love, and go to the land of Moriah, and offer him there as a burnt offering upon one of the mountains of which I shall tell you."

Your son, your only son, Isaac, *whom you love*. Whatever may be said of the origin and provenance of a tale of child sacrifice, the anthropological significance of such a chapter as this fades to the background before these words. To miss their meaning is to miss the point of the whole chapter. This is not a professional priest who is to sacrifice Isaac. This is his father. Nor is this a heartless father who bears no love for his child. This is a father who loves his son. Only a father with the deepest love for his child can proceed beyond this verse to perceive at all the meaning of sin. Whom you love, Abraham, your son, whom you love.

Each generation in ancient Israel knew this story. The children knew it by heart at an early age, and they knew the ram would be in the thicket. But those who knew the meaning of love knew also the meaning of sin, and they listened each time they heard it to trace with Abraham the steps of the three-day journey to Moriah. They knew his heaviness of heart. They felt with him the weight of the wood of sacrifice as he placed it on Isaac. They took with him in their hand the fire and the knife.

"Then Abraham put forth his hand, and took the knife to slay his son." Where else in all literature, save in the passion account of our Lord, is a father's love more painfully, more terribly, more awe-fully portrayed than here. In each generation in Israel this moment of Abraham's love for his son when he lifted his hand to slay him was relived. The terror and the agony was never lost on the heart that knew the meaning of love and the meaning of sin.

But at each telling, that verse was followed by the next, "Abraham, Abraham." The Rabbis say that wherever in the Bible a proper name is thus repeated it means intimate love. "Abraham, Abraham, do not lay your hand on the lad or do anything to him; for now I know that you fear God, seeing you have not withheld your son, your only son, from me."

Abraham did not want to do what God commanded him to do. Does the text say so? No, it says only that Abraham loved his son. He knew the meaning of love and the meaning of sin. Isaac was Abraham's only son, his beloved son, but he was also God's blessing, God's gift. It was no more wrong for Abraham so deeply to love his son than it was for him to accept him as God's gift. Abraham loved this gift of God, this divine blessing; hence, he did not *want* to slay his son, he did not *want* to obey this command to sacrifice his son. But he did obey.

Abraham chose God. He did not have a simple choice, easily discerned, between obvious alternatives. What were the alternatives? The one was the alternative of love, and the other was the alternative of love. What Abraham had to decide was which he loved the more, God's gift or God himself; or, to put it another way, which he feared the more, God in his sovereignty and providence, or his own misgivings about God's sovereignty and providence. For Abraham to fear God was to love him, to cast himself upon the alternative of his providence. The passage cryptically ends, "So Abraham called the name of that place, *YHWH Yir'eh* (the Lord will provide); as it is said to this day 'On the mount of the Lord it will be provided.' "

Later the people of Israel faced the same choice many times. Did they love the promised land, the land flowing with milk and honey, more than they loved God who gave it to them? Their sin, the prophets told them, was in their choice to worship the gift instead of the Giver. They made other gods out of the land and its fertility. They forgot that God had given it to them. They loved God's blessing more than God himself. God's sovereignty and providence was the alternative, the rejected alternative which finally visited them in the form of judgment, exile, and loss of the land they loved, the very gift they mistook and substituted for its giver.

The sin was not in Abraham's loving his son Isaac, nor in Israel's loving the homeland, Canaan. The sin was not in loving God's gifts and blessings but in rejecting God as God. Nor was the sin in being God's creatures, in creatureliness, but in choosing his creation and rejecting him, in loving (or fearing) creation rather than the Creator, the gift rather than the Giver.

Isaiah uses a beautiful love song as an allegory to get the point across about man's responsibility toward the providence of God. The first two verses of Isaiah 5 were undoubtedly a popular love song in Isaiah's day. It was probably sung by the balladiers and professional vocalists, as well as by many young people in his time.

> Let me sing for my beloved
>   a love song concerning his vineyard:
> My beloved had a vineyard
>   on a very fertile hill.
> He digged it and cleared it of stones,
>   and planted it with choice vines;
> he built a watchtower in the midst of it,
>   and hewed out a wine vat in it;
> and he looked for it to yield grapes,
>   but it yielded wild grapes.

This is what we would call today a "blues." It is a song of disappointment. A young swain lovingly plants a vineyard probably thinking to give it to his sweetheart or to support her by means of it in marriage. It is a sad song, a song of bitter sweetness, an ancient "blues."

In the following verses (5:3-6) Isaiah elaborates on the providence of God, first the love of God (3, 4) and then the judgment of God (5, 6). Finally (5:7), as though it were needed, he explains that the vineyard represents Israel and Judah, what God had planted on the fertile hill.

For Isaiah the fertile hill represents Canaan, the so-called promised land. God's gift of the land to Israel is, in the song, a labor of love.

> He digged it and cleared it of stones,
>   and planted it with choice vines;
> he built a watchtower in the midst of it,
>   and hewed out a wine vat in it.

Here the providence of God is a labor of love and Isaiah has God pleading with Israel (verse 4),

> What more was there to do for my vineyard,
>   that I have not done in it?
> When I looked for it to yield grapes,
>   why did it yield wild grapes?

Here is the love of God opening itself to criticism. What love is this that God first asks what more he might have done? This is among those disarming questions God in the depths of his compassion sometimes asks. It is comparable to the question Jeremiah says God asked in a similar situation (Jer. 2:5), "What wrong did your fathers find in me that they went far from me?" Micah, too, says God asked of Israel (Mic. 6:3), "O my people, what have I done to you? In what have I wearied you? Answer me!"

Only men of God like these prophets, who knew the love of God as an unquestioned reality and about which there could be no doubt, could be so daring as to suggest God would thus open himself to Israel's criticism. What have I done wrong? Where was I lacking? God first asks these questions of himself. This is but an indication of the unfathomable depth of the love of God.

Immediately upon the heels of these questions comes the pronouncement of divine judgment (Isa. 5:5, 6):

> And now I will tell you
>   what I will do to my vineyard.
> I will remove its hedge,
>   and it shall be devoured;
> I will break down its wall,
>   and it shall be trampled down.
> I will make it a waste;
>   it shall not be pruned or hoed,
>   and briers and thorns shall grow up;
> I will also command the clouds
>   that they rain no rain upon it.

God declares his judgment on his beloved by withdrawing the blessings of his providence, the hedge and the wall, and by destroying the blessing itself, making of the vineyard a waste. What God had given Israel he converts from a blessing to a curse (cf. Hos. 2:9-13).

Both the blessing and the curse, the gift and its withdrawal, are of the providence or sovereignty of God. There is no biblical evidence whatever to think that God loved Israel less when he judged her than when he blessed her. The love is the same; it does not diminish. The point to note here, as in the case of the story of Abraham and Isaac, is that the gift of God tended to supplant the giver, God himself, in the affections of Israel (Isa. 1:29). Again, there is no reason to think that Israel should not have enjoyed the divine gift. On the contrary, the question is whether or not Israel's commitment was still to God and God alone. Obviously, it was not; for where God had looked for justice (*mishpaṭ*) there was bloodshed (*mispaḥ*), and for righteousness (*tsedaqah*) there was violence (*tse'aqah*) (5:7). They regard the potter as the clay (Isa. 29:16), that is, the giver as the gift; they trust in oppression and perverseness (30:12) rather than in God. They put their faith in creation rather than the Creator (1:29), foreign alliances (31:1-3) and especially a false trust that God is obligated to protect them (28:15, 21; 31:4-5). Isaiah's message centers in that aspect of divine providence which is judgment (1:30, 31; 5:5-6; 6:9-13; 28:16-22, etc.). Even though it is judgment, it is still providence; and in it the love of God is not one whit abated.

Man's sin is his failure in some sense to distinguish between God and his blessings, the Giver and his gifts, the Creator and his creation. The radical distinction established in Genesis 1 between the two categories of being is violated. God's providence or sovereignty is his breaching the same distinction: the Creator is also Lord; he not only creates he rules; he not only gives he takes away; he not only blesses he curses; he not only loves he judges. And in his ruling, in his constant judgment over us, he loves us.

CHAPTER IV

JUDGMENT AND SALVATION

The Bible makes itself quite clear that there is no salvation without judgment. In fact, it goes further and asserts that salvation, or redemption, is in God's judgment. Perhaps in the light of what we have discussed so far it is better to say that judgment is salvation. By this is meant that perspective of faith which understands life in all its facets, life and death, joy and sorrow, victory and defeat, to fall under the sovereignty of God. What else can salvation finally mean, than such a perspective? We never really escape God no matter how successful we become nor how badly we fail. His judgment is ever present; we never get away from it. To know this is salvation.

Salvation is, therefore, the faith-perspective of God's inevitability. It is that which happens to us when we accept God as God, as Lord, truly ruler and judge. The Bible expresses this in a number of ways.

Perhaps the most graphic and even startling of such biblical expressions is a picture Amos draws about "the day of the Lord." In the popular opinion of his time in ancient Israel, the day of the Lord was to be a day of great salvation and glory for Israel. Many Israelites looked forward

to it as a day when God would himself appear on earth
to lead Israel to great victories, when Israel would expand
throughout the known world carrying along her faith in
a successful warrior God. Shocking his hearers, Amos
presented a picture of the day of the Lord as not of light
but of darkness, a day of gloom with no brightness in it
(Amos 5:18-20).

Amos was by trade a shepherd from the poor district
of Tekoa in the Judean wastelands. To get across his
idea of Judgment, the day of the Lord, he drew the people
a picture of what might well happen to a shepherd while
trying to protect his sheep. He used a simile (5:19):

> [It is] as if a man fled from a lion
>   and a bear met him;
> And went into the house and leaned
>   with his hand against the wall and a serpent bit him.

It is not a pretty picture, but it is certainly a clear one.
The shepherd who day by day guards his sheep from
harm is here speaking from personal experience. Giving
chase to a lion who had probably been molesting his flock,
he ran into a bear. Amos compares this fearsome situation to the day of the Lord, to what it means to accept
God as Lord. To be trapped between a lion and a bear
is a real situation. In a situation like that, all one's being is
brought to the surface of what life means. All of life is
brought to a head, as it were. There is no part of it left
behind somewhere to survive. It is all gathered up into
a piece, a unity, a whole.

Out of the corner of his eye the shepherd glimpses his
escape—a house, a hut of some sort. In the nick of time
he realizes his escape. He has eluded both the lion and

the bear—saved! Then in sheer exhaustion he leans for support against an inner wall of the hut, and a serpent bites him!

That, Amos says, is what the day of the Lord means. That is what it means to know God as Lord. Such is Amos' simile, a scene a shepherd would know from intimate experience. Amos' message is for his people in his time: salvation is judgment. Other prophets in other times turned the message around to say that judgment is salvation. It is the same message and the same word of God adapted in differing situations with different emphases: God is Lord, both judge and redeemer, universal and inevitable. There is no escape from him and his reign over us. The people of Israel in Amos' time had begun to feel they had power over God, that God was obliged to honor their victories in his name. Amos had to tell them that the saving God is the judging God, that it was sheer self-deception to vaunt themselves in any way as his elect people.

> Only you have I known
> [entered into a covenant with]
>   of all the families of the earth;
> Therefore will I judge you
>   for all your iniquities.
>   [Amos 3:2]

Amos went so far as to say that Israel was no more to God than the Ethiopians or the Philistines or the Syrians (9:7). Israel had no more to offer God than either her worst enemies or the remotest people. The Bible is quite clear on this matter of election. Israel does not have what other nations lack as a basis of her covenant with God; the covenant was founded because of God's quality to love Israel (Deut. 7:7, 8). Israel's distinctiveness, according to a tradition that is one of the oldest in the Bible and perhaps originating with Moses himself, lies not in herself but in God's own free choice to "go with" Israel (Exod. 33:16). Israel in Amos' time, as well as in the time of other prophets, had deceived herself into thinking herself indispensable, rather than knowing God as inevitable, the Lord whose reign is total. He had to tell them that to know God is to be under his sovereignty; to have a covenant with him is to be judged by him. The covenant did not mean salvation only but also judgment; more than that, it meant that salvation and judgment were synonymous. Moreover; this covenant was not a pact as between equal parties, or one of parity; it was a suzerainty type covenant as between a greater power and a vassal state.[1]

Amos' insistence that there is no escape from the judgment of God is reflected in a poetically less poignant but more beautiful passage in Isaiah. Isaiah was also obligated to set aright the real meaning of the day of the Lord. His problem was like Amos' with a different emphasis. Isaiah had to convince his people that God's judgment knows no barrier, that nothing marked the boundary of his kingdom or the limit of his sovereignty. There is no escape, no place to run for exemption from God's judgment. Nothing in creation, natural or man-made, can provide sufficient shelter against his rule. The effect of his power extends throughout the created order, we would say; it knows no limit. Nothing, no matter how strong or majestic or awe-ful, falls outside his regency.

> For the Lord of hosts has a day
>   against all that is proud and lofty,
>   against all that is lifted up and high;

against all the cedars of Lebanon,
  lofty and lifted up;
  and against all the oaks of Bashan;
against all the high mountains,
  and against all the lofty hills;
against every high tower,
  and against every fortified wall;
against all the ships of Tarshish,
  and against all the beautiful craft.
And the haughtiness of man shall be humbled,
  and the pride of men shall be brought low;
  and the Lord alone will be exalted in that day ...
And men shall enter the caves of the rocks
  and the holes of the ground,
from before the terror of the Lord,
  and from the glory of his majesty,
  when he rises to terrify the earth.

                    [Isa. 2:12-19]

Isaiah puts the majesty of God above every glory of creation. Neither the might nor the power of either nature or man can withstand the power of God. The prophet makes himself equally clear in other passages where he tries to tell his people that no covenant or alliance will shield them from God's effective rule, neither a foreign alliance as with the powerful Egyptian government (30:1-7; 31:1-3) nor Israel's own covenant with God (28:14-22). Isaiah was perhaps most disturbed over the latter, the people's misunderstanding of the covenant. As in Amos' time and even still later in Jeremiah's time, the people considered God obligated to protect them; having a treaty with God shielded them, they felt, from God's righteous judgment. It was one of the major tasks of all the prophets to tell the people of their common self-deception. Their understanding of the covenant was like a bed too short to stretch out in or a blanket too narrow to cover them (Isa. 28:20). The covenant does not protect us from God; it subjects us to his rule. Salvation, our right relation with God, subjects us to his rule. Salvation and judgment are synonymous.

We shall later hear more fully from Jeremiah. For now, let us only listen in on a conversation between Jeremiah and another prophet of his time, Hananiah. Hananiah has just broken a wooden yoke which Jeremiah had worn as a symbol of his conviction that Israel must succumb to the yoke of Babylonian oppression as a disciplinary judgment of God upon her; Hananiah was quite of the opposite conviction and broke the yoke as a sign of his certainty that Jeremiah was wrong and that it would be only a couple of years before those already deported by Nebuchadnezzar would be returned home (Jer. 28:1-2).

Hananiah we call a false prophet. But we do so only because Jeremiah finally says he was. The criteria for distinguishing between true and false prophecy are very nebulous and uncertain. We have no reason to think that false prophets were "bad guys" who were insincere and blackhearted. On the contrary, as "false" as he may have been, Hananiah was as sincere a prophet as Jeremiah. About this the text leaves no doubt. Furthermore, the text clearly shows Jeremiah's own deep respect for Hananiah. After the latter had made his optimistic prediction that all would be well in a couple of years, Jeremiah responded, "Amen! May the Lord do so; may the Lord make the words which you have prophesied come true and bring back to this place from Babylon the vessels of the house of the Lord, and all the exiles" (28:6). This response of Jeremiah's is clearly not a sarcastic one. Jeremiah does not believe Hananiah is right but he in no way impugns his utter sincerity. On the contrary, Jeremiah goes on to discuss the matter with Hananiah. Let us listen in.

Yet hear now this word which I speak in your hearing and in the hearing of all the people. The prophets who preceded you and me from ancient times prophesied war, famine, and pestilence against many countries and great kingdoms. As for the prophet who prophesies peace, when the word of that prophet comes to pass, then it will be known that the Lord has truly sent the prophet.

[28:7-9]

Here it would seem that we have a clear criterion for distinguishing true and false prophecy. The true prophet, Jeremiah would seem to say, can prophesy only hardship and suffering. Manifestly, however, if this is the simple criterion to go by we would have to eliminate much of biblical prophecy. If prophecy of blessing, peace, and prosperity must be corroborated by later evidence to be thought of as divinely endorsed, or a word of God, then much of biblical prophecy is entirely false. Obviously we must look further before arriving at such a simple view.

What we must remember is that it is Jeremiah who is saying this. Jeremiah is the most explicit of the prophets in insisting that judgment is salvation, that God's love is the substance of his disciplinary acts against Israel. He is also the prophet who in his own person experienced the power of God's word both for blessing and for curse. The same word of God is a power both of sweetness and of bitterness (Jer. 15:16-18). It is certainly not one God creating the weal and another the woe (Isa. 45:7). The

Old Testament view of God is the extreme opposite of dualism. Nor is it a different "word of God" in the case of blessing from that of curse. It is the same effective will and rule of God which both saves and judges. On all these points Jeremiah especially is quite adamant. The God who inflicts the wounds of judgment is the same who cures them (Jer. 30:12-17; cf. Isa. 30:20, 26). In the judgment is the salvation, the everlasting love of God (31:2, 3). Out of distress comes the salvation (30:7).[2] Jeremiah was constantly perturbed by those in his day who preached peace without seeing it in the context of God's judging sovereignty (4:10; 6:13, 14; 8:10, 11; 14:13, 14). Such preaching led the people to self-deception (20:6; 23:15-17; 27:10, 14; 29:21, 31).

The peace of God is, in his judgment, his sovereign rule of his people. There is no salvation outside judgment. Rather, salvation, the true salvation from God, comes in the acceptance of the awe-ful sovereignty of God. God both judges and saves; one cannot be had without the other. For Jeremiah, as for his predecessors Amos and Isaiah, God's sovereignty is universal or inevitable. It is inescapable. There is no running or hiding from it. Even those taken into exile in a foreign country are still under the rule of God. God is in no sense limited by national boundaries. Jeremiah writes a letter to those who have been deported to Babylonia in 597 B.C., exhorting them to pray to Yahweh there, even to pray for the welfare of the Babylonians (29:7). Jeremiah explains that those who were sent into exile are the blessed ones, the "good figs" (24:4-7), while those who escaped deportation and were "lucky" enough to stay home are those who are under judgment, "the bad figs" (24:8-10). In other words, those who are in exile and thus are considered unfortunate are saved, while those who seemingly escaped and are considered fortunate are judged. The judged are saved and the saved are judged.

What Jeremiah says to Hananiah now makes very good sense. Jeremiah wants peace also. He loves his people. He does not of himself desire suffering for them. He hopes Hananiah is right. "Amen! May the Lord do so." But Jeremiah knows that there is no peace or wholeness or salvation outside judgment, and he therefore knows Hananiah is wrong, even if he himself would have it otherwise.

The inevitability of the sovereignty of God is fully expressed in Psalm 139. God's judgment here is seen as a constant inescapable scrutiny.

> O Lord, thou hast searched me and known me!
> Thou knowest when I sit down and when I arise;
>   thou discernest my thoughts from afar.
> Thou searchest out my path and my bed,
>   and art acquainted with all my ways.
> Even before a word is on my tongue,
>   lo, O Lord, thou knowest it altogether.
> Thou dost beset me behind and before,
>   and layest thy hand upon me.
> Such knowledge is too wonderful for me;
>   it is high, I cannot grasp it.
>
> Whither shall I go from thy Spirit?
>   Or wither shall I flee from thy presence?
> If I ascend to heaven, thou art there!
>   If I make my bed in sheol, thou art there!
> If I take the wings of the morning
>   and dwell in the uttermost parts of the sea,
> even there thy hand shall lead me,
>   and thy right hand shall hold me.

If I say, "Let only darkness cover me,
   and the light about me be night,"
even the darkness is not dark to thee,
   the night is as bright as day;
for darkness is as light with thee.

[Ps. 139:1-12]

"Thou dost beset me behind and before." There is no escape from God. But this is not the simple observation that one never escapes creation or the evidence of God's handiwork. This besetting fore and aft is a dogging scrutiny. God is Lord always and everywhere. His sovereignty is never and nowhere relaxed. It is a probing, searching rule of God which never lets go. This is at least as terrible a thing as Jeremiah's insistence on war, famine, and pestilence as the prophetic message. There is no escape from this "hounding" which the Psalmist experiences, just as there was none for the shepherd in Amos' illustration or for any man as in Isaiah's proclamation. Even death, the Psalmist knows, will not release him. There is absolutely no flight, no deliverance, no salvation from the awful sovereignty of God. "Even the darkness is not dark to thee." When one begins to perceive as does this Psalmist what it means that "God is with us," he begins to know both the saving and the judging aspect of his presence. As we have seen, God told Moses that Israel's distinctiveness was that God would go with them (Exod. 33:16). Isaiah's idea of Immanuel, "God with us," lies at the heart of biblical thought (Isa. 7:14). But it is deceptive to think of this concept as one of comfort only. As the prophets constantly warned, it is a frightening concept as well. There is no escape.

Paul, in the New Testament, sums up the idea:

Who shall separate us from the love of Christ? Shall tribulation, or distress, or persecution, or famine, or nakedness, or peril, or sword? . . . No, in all these things we are more than conquerors, through him who loved us. For I am sure that neither death, nor life, nor angels, nor principalities, nor things present, nor things to come, nor powers, nor height, nor depth, nor anything else in all creation, will be able to separate us from the love of God in Christ Jesus our Lord.

[Romans 8:35-39]

Even in tribulation there is the love of God? How can the love of God be present in distress, persecution, famine, peril, the sword, and all the rest? And yet that is precisely what Paul says. He is saying what we have seen the Old Testament say. The love of God is not a guarantor of sweetness and light. The Bible nowhere suggests that because God loves us we have escaped reality. Of course, it is a comfort to know that nothing in all creation, that is of the created order (and only God is not of the created order), can separate us from God's love. But there is absolutely no suggestion that God's love assures prosperity and peace. The only comfort there is, is in the faith-knowledge that we cannot be cut off from God's transforming love by anything whatever.

And that is frightening in itself! Is there no vacation from the love of God? None. Can't I accuse God of not being God when I get hurt? Absolutely not. Nothing, categorically nothing, offers escape from God's love. It will pursue us to every corner of life's experiences. It will hound us every moment of every circumstance. Can't I escape into doubt and skepticism? No, for the love of God seems to beset us hardest in our honest doubts. Such a concept of complete, total universality is, as the Psalmist says, knowledge too wonderful for us to grasp. This love reaches the worst and the best we know. No matter how greatly we succeed or how badly we fail there is no passport to another kingdom, or another state. The kingdom of God, that state of faith-knowledge of the universal sovereignty of God, has no boundaries to contain it. God alone is its king and he rules forever, judging and saving and loving. I cannot buy my way out by doing good; I cannot get myself expelled by doing evil. That was the lesson Job had to learn. Even our best, our goodness, our piety, our obedience, and our righteousness will not exempt us from the judgment of God. In his kingdom we try to obey God because he loves us, not because we do not want him to be God anymore. We cannot buy with obedience our freedom from his judgment. Nor by disobedience do we forfeit the love of God. Nothing, nothing, nothing can separate us from the all-pervading sovereignty of God.

The great bulk of the prophetic message in the Old Testament is made up of two pronouncements: the prophets declaim the people's sin, and they announce the punishment which under the sovereignty of a just and ethical God must follow. For the prophets there is no need to debate the simple formula: sins bring punishment. The corollary is that obedience brings blessings and much of the prophetic message is made up of pleadings with the people to repent. But the prophets all realized sooner or later in their ministry that simple confession of sins and repentance by rote were more injurious to the people than no repentance at all, and hence were forced to the position of wanting, as prophets, what as normal warm-blooded men among men they could not desire for their people—the wound of blessing, or as we have seen, the judgment that brings salvation.

Isaiah's experience in this regard is the most poignant. He frequently in his forty years (*ca.* 740-700 B.C.) of prophetic ministry pleaded with his people and even argued with them.

> Come now, let us reason together,
>   says the Lord:
> If your sins are like scarlet,
>   can they be as white as snow?
> If they are red as crimson,
>   can they become like wool?
>   [Isa. 1:18]

This is, so to speak, the topic for debate. Then Isaiah provides the axis for the discussion:

> If you are willing and obedient,
>   you shall eat the good of the land;
> But if you refuse and rebel,
>   you shall be devoured by the sword. . . .
>   [Isa. 1:19, 20]

Nothing could be clearer: obedience brings blessings, disobedience brings curses. This same principle is the axis of the law codes in the Old Testament. At the end of the various codes of law are listed the blessings that ensue on obedience to the law and the curses that disobedience will provoke (Exod. 23:20-33; Deut. 27-30; Lev. 26). The Sermon on the Mount in Matthew, which in literary form is patterned after these Old Testament law codes, also ends with a section on the consequences of obedience and disobedience (Matt. 7:24-27).

Thus Isaiah early in his ministry often pleaded with the people to repent. In the terrible days of the siege of

Jerusalem, in 701 B.C., he summed up for the people what he had for some forty years been exhorting them to do. "This is rest: give rest to the weary; this is repose" (28:12). The words "rest" and "repose" (*menuḥah* and *marge'ah*) mean salvation or security. It was the same sort of thing he had told King Ahaz back in 734 B.C. when the king had been gravely concerned about the threat of invasion by the Syro-Ephraimitic alliance, the countries of Syria and northern Israel. "If you do not have faith you will surely not be established [or, be made secure]" (7:9). Perhaps the most familiar of Isaiah's exhortations is the one in 30:15, "In repentance and rest will you be saved; in calmness and trust will be your strength." Isaiah's calm center of faith is in many ways a focal point for any biblical understanding of faith.

Something very bitter, however, enters into Isaiah's later ministry. Even in the verse which sums up his pleas for repentance and faith, there is deep disappointment expressed, "Yet they would not hear" (28:12). There is evidence for thinking that Isaiah experienced real disillusionment over the sincerity of repentance. The people evidently did heed Isaiah at times, perhaps in moments of stress and of threat to their national and personal security, and did repent. But the prophet was able to see in their confession of sin and of faith a shocking falsehood.

Because this people draw near with their mouth
  and honor me with their lips,
  while their hearts are far from me,
  and their fear of me is a commandment of men learned by
    rote;
Therefore, behold I will again do marvelous things with this people,

wonderful and marvelous;
and the wisdom of their wise men shall perish,
and the discernment of their discerning men shall be hid.

[Isa. 29:13, 14]

The prophet was eventually forced to realize that all
his pleas for repentance had boomeranged. The people's
self-deception is now rooted so deeply that preaching for
repentance is no longer possible. On the contrary, when
they repent they but deceive themselves into thinking all
is well. How easy it is to do as the prophet has bade them
do! Surely, we will repent, say the people, that's easy!
and so they go through the ceremony of confession and
nothing, absolutely nothing, has changed. Except that
they stupify themselves into thinking that thereby they
have discharged the full obligation.

It was when the prophet realized what his pleas for
repentance had wrought that he himself was shocked
into the most radical kind of thinking.

> Stupefy yourselves and be in a stupor;
>   blind yourselves and be blind!
> Be drunk, but not with wine;
>   stagger, but not with strong drink!
> For the Lord has poured out upon you
>   a spirit of deep sleep,
> and has closed your eyes, the prophets,
>   and covered your heads, the seers.

[Isa. 29:9, 10]

"The Lord has poured out upon you a spirit of deep
sleep." Isaiah attributes to God the fact that the people
are so completely stupefied and duped. God has used the
prophets to stupefy and deceive the people. This verse
(29:10) is usually understood as an indictment against
false prophets. Rather, it is quite clear that the prophet

is referring even to himself. God has used him in his preaching repentance to dupe the people. God wanted the people to go through the experience of rote repentance and see that it would not avert his judgment. They had thought that repentance averted God's judgment. Now they must learn that repentance affirms God's judgment.

This is a radical turn in the prophet's thinking. He begins to move out of his despair, over the people's self-deception in their ceremonies of rote repentance, into a new perspective. Even this is of God. Even this impossible state of utter stupor in the people is part of God's plan. The people must experience God's judgment so that they will know his salvation. The prophet is beginning to realize that only in judgment is salvation truly of God.

Isaiah becomes so convinced of his new conviction that, in reflecting on his call to the ministry back in his youth, he sees that from the beginning it had been God's purpose that he deceive the people by preaching repentance to them so that they would do as they have actually done, effect a meaningless confession by rote, thus sinking deeper and deeper into their stupor and blindness. To what end, for what purpose? So that they would come to know the reality, the totality, the universality of God's sovereignty; so that they would come to know God's judgment.

And I heard the voice of the Lord saying, "Whom shall I send, and who will go for us?" Then I said, "Here I am! Send me." And he said, "Go, and say to this people:
  'Hear and hear, but do not understand;
     see and see, but do not perceive.'
  Make the heart of this people fat,
     and their ears heavy,
     and shut their eyes;

lest they see with their eyes,
  and hear with their ears,
and understand with their hearts,
  and turn and be healed."
Then I said, "How long, O Lord?"
And he said:
"Until cities lie waste without inhabitant,
and houses without men,
  and the land is utterly desolate,
and the Lord removes men far away,
  and the forsaken places are many in the midst of the land.
And though a tenth remain in it,
  it will be burned again,
like a terebinth or an oak,
  whose stump remains standing when it is felled."
                                                    [Isa. 6:8-13]

What faith is this the prophet exhibits! And what hope! This is plainly not a passage of despondency or despair but one of radical hope. Isaiah will preach repentance so that the people will repent; but it is a false repentance, empty of meaning, a thing learned of men by rote. It will serve but to blind them so that they are further from "understanding" and "perceiving" than ever, further from a true repentance which heals than ever. Isaiah then asks of God how long such falsehood must persist. It must persist until judgment is complete, until the people see that God's sovereignty is universal. It will be a total 100 per cent judgment. The judgment itself will last until even when the country is decimated, the final tenth, the stump left standing, will experience God's total rule. Judgment is clearly not a game of percentages. It is total; it is a 100 per cent affair. There can be no thought of escape from it by anyone. If, for instance, judgment stopped at the 90 per cent mark, one can be sure the people would all consider themselves worthy of being in the 10 per cent "remnant" left unjudged. No, the judgment is total and complete.

And that is the hope! For this is ultimately a passage of great hope. The hope is in the judgment, in the 100 per cent rule and sovereignty of God. Outside God's judgment there is no hope.

The judgment will effect what repentance cannot effect. The judgment will be nonselective. The judgment will pre-empt any false repentance; it will render void any possibility of the people's deceiving themselves into thinking they have bought God off with shallow superficial acts of worship and sacrifice. Isaiah is particularly disturbed over those who simulate acts of worship totally without any depth of conviction that God is truly the God whose regency is real and whose sovereignty touches life to its furtherest bounds.

> What to me is the multitude of your sacrifices?
>   says the Lord.
> I have had enough of burnt offerings of rams
>   and the fat of fed beasts.
> I do not delight in the blood of bulls,
>   or of lambs, or of he-goats.
> When you come to appear before me,
>   who requires of you
>   this trampling of my courts?
> Bring no more vain offerings;
>   incense is an abomination to me . . .
> When you spread forth your hands,
>   I will hide my eyes from you;
> even though you make many prayers,
>   I will not listen.
> Your hands are full of blood.
>   [Isa. 1:11-13, 15]

As long as the people feel they can pacify God with rite and ceremony they also feel they can escape the realm of his reign and thus the consequences of their evil deeds. The formula is simple: keep God pacified and so limit his power.

> Woe to those who hide deep from the Lord their counsel,
>   whose deeds are in the dark,
>   and who say, "Who sees us? Who knows us?"
> You turn things upside down!
>   Shall the potter be regarded as the clay;
> that the creature may say of its creator,
>   "He did not make me";
> or the thing formed say of him who formed it,
>   "He has no understanding"?
>
> [Isa. 29:15-16]

False repentance and false piety can lead to a nearly total denial of the sovereignty of God. There were among the people even those who dared to challenge God to do something, anything at all, so little faith was left.

> Let him make haste,
>   let him speed his work
>   that we may see it.
> Let the purpose of the Holy one of Israel draw near;
>   let it come, that we may know it!
>
> [Isa. 5:19]

So long as God honored the people's repenting, even a repentance that for a moment was sincere, the people lost the sense of his lordship, his sovereignty and power. They succumbed to a stupor. They felt they had God in a box, bound and strapped. Into such a situation Isaiah knew that divine judgment must enter to shake the foundations and turn things right side up. The people even began to think of the land as holy, the city as holy, and the temple as holy, special places God would always protect. They, in their stupor, believed that God had committed himself to defend the "holy city." They had a favorite saying they comforted themselves with even as the Assyrians began to lay waste the Judean countryside, and Isaiah quotes it in utter contempt:

> Like birds hovering, so the Lord of hosts
>   will protect Jerusalem;
> he will protect and deliver it,
>   he will spare and rescue it.
>
> [Isa. 31:5][8]

The people had begun to worship and revere the city as holy, particularly because of the presence of the temple within it. Because of their misunderstanding of the Davidic covenant they got the notion that the city was inviolable, that it was completely impossible to harm it. They had begun to think of it as a sanctuary with its sanctuary, the temple as the safeguard in its midst. Isaiah fought the idea of the inviolability of the city and the sacredness of the temple with might and main. God one day warned him.

> Do not call binding all this people call binding and do not fear what they fear [revere], nor be in dread. But the Lord of hosts, *him* you shall regard as holy; let him be your fear, and let him be your dread.
>
> [Isa. 8:12, 13]

Nothing is holy but God! Nothing is sacred but God! Nothing is to be revered or feared but God! Certainly not a city nor a temple! They are equally as liable to the power of his judgment as all else in creation. The people had begun to substitute a created thing for the Creator, to let the temple supplant God. Isaiah tried to get the people to understand that absolutely nothing is holy but God, that God does not need the temple or the city to be God.

> And *he* will become a sanctuary . . .
> [Isa. 8:14]

Isaiah pleads with the people to let God be their sanctuary. A sanctuary is a place in which to escape. The people's stupor was in thinking that the temple would afford escape from God himself. Let God be your sanctuary!

> . . . and a stone of offence, and a rock of stumbling to both houses of Israel, a trap and a snare to the inhabitants of Jerusalem. And many shall stumble thereon; they shall fall and be broken; they shall be snared and taken.
> [Isa. 8:14, 15; cf. 28:13]

Here is succinctly stated the most difficult part of the prophetic message; both the judgment and the hope are seen in the same act of God against and for the people. God himself will be a trap and a snare, a stumbling block on which the people will fall and be broken. They will be snared and taken by God who at the same time is Israel's only sanctuary, or avenue of salvation. God will cause them to stumble into his own arms, as it were. God will snare them and entrap them in the sanctuary of his own love and sovereignty. The judgment is the salvation. Isaiah repeats the idea but with the emphasis this time on the redemption.

> Thus says the Lord God, "Behold I am laying in Zion for a foundation a stone, a tested stone, a precious cornerstone of a sure foundation: 'He who has faith will not be in a frenzy.'"
> [Isa. 28:16]

The stumbling stone is also a foundation stone or a corner-stone. It is understood as such by the man of faith: the judgment is the salvation.

Hosea had said much the same thing when he too insisted that God's judgment of Israel was for the purpose of salvation. God says,

> I will return again to my place,
>   until they acknowledge their guilt and seek my face,
>   and in their distress they seek me, saying,
> "Come, let us return to the Lord;
>   for he has torn, that he may heal us;
>   he has stricken, and he will bind us up. . . ."
>
> [Hos. 5:15-6:1]

God tears in order to heal. He who strikes is the same as he who binds up. But we sadly miss the point if we see that God so delights in healing and binding up that he tears and smites in order to do so. Rather it must be seen clearly that the healing begins with the smiting. Though the analogy is poor, consider the work of the surgeon. The operation for cure does not begin with binding up or sewing up the incision; it begins with the incision itself. The smiting is for healing; the judgment is for salvation.

Hosea draws the analogy of God's relation to Israel from his own experience with his wife. In the analogy Hosea is as God and Gomer is as Israel. Hosea's marriage to Gomer had its similarities to God's covenant with Israel. Just as Gomer was undoubtedly a fine, clean girl when Hosea married her so Israel was a nation whom God could love; as the prophet says, Israel was like "grapes in the wilderness" when God found her, like "the first fruit on the fig tree" (9:10; cf. 11:1). But, just as Gomer became harlotrous and unfaithful to Hosea, so Israel became

apostate and unfaithful to God; as the prophet says, Israel
began to sin when she had entered Canaan, the promised land
(9:10, 15; 11:2; 13-1, 2, 4-6).[4]

The answer to the problem of Gomer's relation to
Hosea, as well as the solution to the disrupted or sin-
ridden relation of Israel to God, is found in Hosea, Chapter 2. There the figures of the analogy are mixed. Gomer
and Israel are referred to simultaneously. Hosea's action
against Gomer to restrain her from her harlotries is read as
God's disciplinary judgment against Israel (2:6-13). Then
the prophet explains the purpose of the judgment:

Therefore, behold, I will allure her,
    and bring her into the wilderness,
    and speak tenderly to her.
And there I will give her her vineyards,
    and make the valley of Achor a door of hope.
And there she shall answer as in the days of her youth,
    as at the time when she came out of the land of Egypt.
                                        [Hos. 2:14, 15]

God's alluring Israel into the wilderness is the figure of
the judgment, deprivation of the blessings of the gift of
the land, the good things of the promise. But God's judgment is never an end in itself for these prophets. Judgment
is redemption; for there in the wilderness God will speak
tenderly to Israel. Here is seen the loving purpose of God
in the judgment. In the judgment God loves his people.
The Hebrew expression here translated "speak tenderly
to her" literally says "speak upon her heart." God in the
judgment enters into a new covenant with his people. It
is an intimate covenant of love wrought of the harshness
of judgment. God's love is seen by the prophet as so great
that he says God will restore the vineyards of the promised

land, which the judgment has itself deprived them of, right there in the desert.

Extremely important is Israel's response. "There she shall answer as in the days of her youth." Israel will enter into the covenant with God. She will in the midst of the judgment, the desert, perceive that the judgment is of God, that it is God who has brought the calamity upon them. Israel in judgment confesses the sovereignty of God. This is not just another case of adversity on the wheel of fortune. On the contrary, the one truly righteous God has, in his love for his people, judged them.

God's outreach in the judgment is accepted by Israel. Israel says her "Yes!" to God's grace in judgment. The two are necessary to any understanding that judgment is salvation: God's initiative and the people's response. No longer then is judgment an end in itself, or adversity or suffering a cause for despair. Rather, God has entered Israel's suffering and transformed her valley of trouble or Achor into a door of hope. The hope is in the judgment. God speaks tenderly in suffering, or upon the naked heart of his people, and despair is transformed into hope.

If the people do respond, or can perceive that this is not just another case of defeat and adversity but rather that God is tenderly speaking to them, so harshly, then the new covenant will be effected.

And in that day, says the Lord, you will call me, "My husband," and no longer will you call me, "My Baal." For I will remove the names of the Baals from her mouth, and they shall be mentioned by name no more. . . . And I will betroth you to me for ever; I will betroth you to me in righteousness and in justice, in steadfast love, and in mercy. I will betroth you to me by faith that you may know the Lord.

[Hos. 2:16, 17, 19, 20]

CHAPTER V

JUDGMENT AND SALVATION
continued

The harshness of God's speaking tenderly is nowhere more clearly seen than in Jeremiah. Jeremiah time and again informs the people both of the coming judgment and of its purpose. The judgment will be a terrible experience, a time of distress incomparable in Israel's experience.

> We have heard a cry of panic,
>   of terror and of no peace.
> Ask now, and consider,
>   can a man bear a child?
> Why then do I see every man
>   with his hands on his loins like a woman in labor?
>   Why has every face turned pale?
> Alas! that day is so great
>   there is none like it.
> It is a time of distress for Jacob;
>   but out of it will come his salvation.[1]
>
> > [Jer. 30:5-7]

The time of distress is the moment of judgment and Jeremiah here compares it to the distress and suffering that a woman experiences in childbirth. Out of the labor pains will issue salvation. Jeremiah clearly interprets judgment as the process of redemption. This is the harsh tenderness of the figure in Hosea we have just seen.

Jeremiah like the other prophets uses the figure of wounds to describe the judgment God inflicts. Isaiah refers to the judgment as sickness, bruises, sores, and bleeding wounds (Isa. 1:5, 6), Micah speaks of the incurable wound of God's judgment which in his time reached to the very gates of Jerusalem (Micah 1:9). Both Isaiah and Micah had particular reference to Assyria's siege of Jerusalem in 701 B.C., which they consistently interpreted as divine judgment on Judah.

Jeremiah also speaks of the incurable wound of God's judgment. God smites his people in order to draw them to him. When they experience the smiting quite naturally they seek some cure for the wound. The people in Jeremiah's time no more chose to believe their God would hurt them than we choose to believe he would today. Popular belief in every age is that God protects and comforts. The awful task of the prophets was to tell the people that their God was judging them. It is the awful task of the church today to bear the same message; it is the eternal message of the cross but like the people of Jeremiah's time we deny God in the adversity.

> Is there no balm in Gilead?
>   Is there no physician there?
> Why then has the health of the daughter of my people
>   not been restored?
>
> [Jer. 8:22]

The wound of judgment is incurable. Of course, there is balm in Gilead. Gilead was renowned for the balm that was made from the resin of the Styrax tree which grew there in abundance. Many self-styled physicians made a business of administering the balm. But the people's health is still not restored. No external balm will cure the God-inflicted wounds. The wounds of judgment are incurable wounds.

> For thus says the Lord:
> Your hurt is incurable,
>   and your wound is grievous.
> There is none to uphold your cause,
>   no medicine for your wound,
>   no healing for you.
>
> [Jer. 30:12, 13]

There is no way whatever to deny the wounds of judgment. These are the wounds of God's own doing; they cannot be wished away.

> All your lovers have forgotten you;
>   they care nothing for you;
> for I have dealt you the blow of an enemy,
>   a harsh discipline,
> because your guilt is great,
>   because your sins are flagrant.
> Why do you cry out over your hurt?
>   Your pain is incurable.
> Because your guilt is great,
>   because your sins are flagrant,
>   I have done these things to you.
>
> [Jer. 30:14, 15]

God has assumed the role of an enemy to Israel in order to judge his people (Isa. 1:24). It is God who has dealt the blow. He it was who smote his people. He has judged them for their sins. However, even though he has seemingly assumed the role of an enemy he loves his people none the less.

> Is Ephraim my dear son?
>   Is he my darling child?
> For as often as I speak against him,
>   I do remember him still.
> Therefore my heart yearns for him;
>   I will surely have mercy on him.
>   [Jer. 31:20]

God, because he loves his people, disciplines them and judges them to redeem them. The God-inflicted wound is incurable. Nothing in the created order will heal the wound or restore the health of Israel under judgment. Only the very one who inflicted the wounds can heal them.

> For I will restore health to you,
>   and your wounds I will heal.
>   [Jer. 30:17]

The emphasis is on the pronoun "I." Neither balms nor lovers (Israel's political allies) are effective to cure what God alone can heal. The enemy was no enemy at all. God who had acted like an enemy in the judgment loved dearly the son he was disciplining. The smiter is the healer. The smiting becomes the healing, the judgment the salvation. The God who inflicted the wound is the same God who heals them (cf. Isa. 30:20, 26). He loves his people through every moment of the judgment. As Isaiah had put it, God wanted to snare them and trap them and cause them to fall—right into his own arms.

The instrument of God's judgment upon his people in 597 B.C. and again in 587 B.C. was Babylonia. Under Nebuchadnezzar Babylonia totally defeated Judah and razed Jerusalem and the temple. Both in 597 and in 587 and even again in 582 the Babylonians deported many people of Judah and exiled them to Babylonia. The whole terrible story is told in II Kings 24-25, II Chronicles 36, and Jeremiah 37-44. Jeremiah, who had been imprisoned during the siege of Jerusalem, was released by the captain of Nebuchadnezzar's bodyguard, Nebuzaradan, by the Babylonian king's own order (Jer. 39:11-14). Nebuzaradan then gave Jeremiah his choice as to whether he should go to Babylonia or stay in Judah. Jeremiah chose to stay in Judah where he firmly believed God's blessing for his people would again be manifest. During the siege Jeremiah had bought a field in his home town Anathoth from his cousin Hanamel (32:6-15). Hanamel had come to him while he was in prison during the siege, beseeching Jeremiah to buy the field from him since the right of redemption had fallen to the prophet by heritage. Hanamel was cleverly getting rid of his property rights in exchange for money. During the siege, one can be sure, inflation had seized Jerusalem's dwindling markets, and prices had risen to a point that a great deal of money was needed to purchase food. Hanamel, like everyone else, knew that property rights would probably be worthless under Babylonian domination. He figured easily to gain if he could sell his field. Jeremiah, his cousin, was just the man to approach. With the battle going so obviously to the Babylonians Hanamel would have been hard put to sell to any normal businessman of means to purchase.

Jeremiah was, of course, no normal businessman. He immediately agreed to purchase the field, and in order to make a prophetic point of the transaction, went through all of the legal procedures normal for peaceful times. He had two deeds of purchase made out, got witnesses to sign them and asked Baruch, his amanuensis, to put them in earthenware vessels that they might last a long time. All this, in view of the circumstances, was rather absurd. Jeremiah did it all to make the point, "Houses and fields and vineyards shall again be bought in this land" (32:15). In the midst of the siege Jeremiah spoke of hope and redemption, just as earlier in the days of prosperity he had spoken of judgment.

Jeremiah, as we have seen, elected to stay in Judah once the catastrophe of judgment had befallen his people. A few others were permitted to stay also. But most of the population not already deported in 597 B.C. were exiled to Babylonia. We can picture the scene of long files of people being herded out of Jerusalem to start the hard weary trek north and then eastward to Babylonia. Let us suppose that Jeremiah stands watching his neighbors and friends, his very own people, emerging through the Damascus Gate, guarded and guided by Nebuzaradan and his soldiers, going out into the wilderness of homelessness and banishment (Jer. 52:12-30). The full measure of God's judgment is upon them, as Jeremiah had said it would be.

Jeremiah stands watching them as they go and once more speaks to them:

> Thus says the Lord:
> The people who have survived the sword
>   have found grace in the desert,
> Israel going to his rest.
>   From afar the Lord appears to him, saying,
> "With an everlasting love have I loved you;
>   now shall I extend to you my *ḥesed*."
>   [Jer. 31:2, 3][2]

Those "who have survived the sword" are for the prophet not only these being taken into exile who perchance did not perish in the battle, they are the surviving people of

Israel who emerge on the other side of the sword to perceive that it is not just Nebuchadnezzar who has wielded the sword but God himself who has judged them. Unless they have this faith-perception that this is not just another case of the fortunes of history wherein a larger army and nation have defeated a smaller one, but rather that even in defeat God is sovereign, then there has been no judgment and hence no salvation. There must be the people's response. Judgment is not automatic in adversity. Jeremiah later in the same chapter insists on this point of the people's response or faith-perception (Jer. 31:18, 19; cf. Hos. 2:14-15; 6:1).

Those, then, who accept the judgment find "grace in the desert, Israel going to his rest." The word "rest" here as elsewhere in the Old Testament means security or salvation. The "desert" here again signifies the judgment, the realities of which the people are so acutely experiencing. Hence, Jeremiah is here at the moment of the calamity asserting what he has all along been preaching: in the judgment is salvation. Emerging into that desert of judgment the people "who have survived the sword," those who recognize and accept the sovereignty of God even in the adversity of catastrophe, will see God. God appears to them from afar to say, "I have loved you with an everlasting love." Does Jeremiah mean that God's love was present even in the worst of the calamity? Yes! He had not for a moment ceased to love them. Because he loved them he disciplined them and judged them in order to grant them his salvation. Judgment is salvation.

God's plan and purpose for his people goes far beyond salvation in judgment. He saves them for a purpose. Jeremiah expressed this purpose as a new covenant wherein the people would become a people of prophets, a prophetic people. They, like the prophets, will now have the word of God, his will for them, his *torah*, written on their hearts. Whereas heretofore there had been a prophetic movement within Israel, there would now be a prophetic Israel within the world (Jer. 31:31-34).[3]

Jeremiah himself does not fully develop the idea of the prophetic Israel and its role within the world. That is left to his successor whom we call the Second Isaiah, or Deutero-Isaiah, whose message is found in Isaiah, chapters 40-55.

The Second Isaiah prophesied in Babylonia around the year 538 B.C., right at the time when Babylonia was defeated by Persia. Cyrus, the victorious king of Persia, freed the captive peoples under the Babylonian yoke and permitted the Jews to return to Judah (II Chron. 36:22, 23; Ezra 1:2-4). These events, obviously favorable to the Jews, afforded the setting for the ministry of this exilic prophet whose message is the complement to the messages of pre-exilic prophets. It is the full statement of the meaning of the salvation which came to Judah in judgment. It should not be understood as a contrast to the prophetic message of judgment but rather its full outcome, its climax.

The Second Isaiah preached hope and salvation. Whereas his predecessors had spoken of judgment primarily, he spoke of salvation primarily. But just as Hosea and Isaiah and Jeremiah had interpreted the judgment as purposeful, as an awful step toward salvation, so must this later prophet relate his message of hope and redemption to the foregoing judgment. His main task was really the same as theirs had been, to show the necessary relation of salvation to judgment. To be sure, the Second Isaiah begins his message with the proclamation that the suffering and the adverse aspects of the judgment were finished:

> Comfort, comfort my people,
> 　says your God.
> Speaks tenderly to Jerusalem,
> 　and cry to her
> that her sentence is ended,
> 　that her iniquity is pardoned,
> that she has received from the Lord's hand
> 　double for all her sins.
>
> 　　　　　　　　　　　　　[Isa. 40:1-2]

And what a glorious proclamation! The people who have for some fifty years been subservient to the yoke of Babylonian domination hear the good news of redemption: We are going home! For the occasion the prophet composes what is comparable to a symphony wherein the desert is pictured as yielding its almost impassable terrain to a magnificent highway. Valleys will be lifted up and mountains brought low and rough places made plain (Isa. 40:3-4). The symphony reaches its crescendo and allegretto when the prophet brings into it a mighty chorus:

> For you shall go out in joy,
> 　and be led forth in peace;
> the mountains and the hills before you
> 　shall break forth into singing,
> 　and all the trees of the field shall clap their hands.
>
> 　　　　　　　　　　　　　[Isa. 55:12]

But even at the very beginning the prophet makes reference to the judgment. It was from the Lord's hand that Israel had suffered so much. That must not be forgotten in the delight of hearing the message of salvation and its accompanying symphony (40:2).

He emphasizes the point several times in his ministry.

> Who gave up Jacob to the spoiler
> and Israel to the robbers?
> Was it not the Lord against whom we have sinned?
>
> [Isa. 42:24]

> For a brief moment I forsook you,
> but with great compassion I will gather you.
> In overflowing wrath for a moment
> I hid my face from you,
> but with everlasting love I will have compassion on you,
> says the Lord, your Redeemer.
>
> [Isa. 54:7, 8]

He who is now redeeming is the same who formerly judged. Redemption then is not God's snatching his people from some evil over which he has no control. Redemption is a divine sequel to judgment. God brought the judgment in order to redeem his people. The full relationship of the salvation to the judgment is established time and again as in Isaiah 43:25-28 through 44:8. Israel is God's witness, both to his righteousness in judgment and his grace in salvation.

Israel, as God's witness (Isa. 43:10-13), has borne God's judgment for the world to see. That was the startling message of the earlier prophets. God is God precisely because he judges his own people whom he loves. The popular notion among all peoples in polytheism had been that a god who had any power at all would, of course, prosper his people, fight their battles for them, and generally show his mettle. There is evidence that many Jews in exile held such a popular notion and doubted that the Lord was any longer powerful (Isa. 40:27). After all, if Babylonia had defeated Israel then the gods of Babylonia had manifestly bested the Lord himself (Isa. 46:1-13). There is also evidence that many Jews went over to worship the Babylonian gods (Isa. 50:11).[4] This, we must understand, was the normal thing for the defeated Jews to believe. The task of the prophet was to show how God had manifested himself in judgment.

The method of the Second Isaiah to get at his problem is to posit a debate between Israel, the people of God, and all nations who worship other gods. He calls for the debate in chapter 41 and it continues almost throughout his message. God is truly God and Lord, that is, the one sovereign, universal, monotheistic God, precisely because he righteously judged his own people. The proof of it is in history. Isaiah's debate has rightly been called the argument from prophecy to montheism, prophecy here meaning the prophetic view of history.[5] Israel has borne God's judgment for the world to observe therein God's sovereign righteousness and God's witnesses the prophets declared it so in his name. Now, at the time of this prophet, Israel is bearing God's blessing of salvation for the world to observe.[6] Israel he also calls "a covenant to the people, a light to the nations" (42:6; 49:8). The significance of what God has done is not limited to the interests of Israel alone; it extends to the ends of the world. All nations of the world, frequently poetically called "coastlands" by our prophet, are invited to engage in the debate and to see what God has done in his people Israel.

> The coastlands have seen and are afraid,
>   the ends of the earth tremble;
>   they have drawn near and come.
> [Isa. 41:5]

The nations are invited to present the case for their gods and to have their gods interpret the past or declare what is to come. Therein lies the proof. For the Lord, who is the one true God, has from antiquity interpreted history, past, present and future, through his prophets. But the idols can effect neither blessing nor curse, judgment nor salvation, and are hence nothing (41:21-24; 43:9; 45:20-21).

The whole world would be utterly dumbfounded to understand the truth.

> Kings shall see and arise;
>> Princes, and they shall prostrate themselves . . .
>>> [Isa. 49:7]

The protocol of royalty will be disrupted. Kings, who remain seated on their thrones and rise for no one, will stand up. And princes, who are accustomed to have others prostrate before them, will prostrate themselves before the truth of the saving acts of God. Israel, God's witness, is his suffering servant, in whom God has manifested his glory both for judgment and salvation.

> Behold, my servant shall prosper,
>> he shall be exalted and lifted up,
>> and shall be very high.
> As many were astonished at him—
>> his appearance was so marred, beyond human semblance,
>> and his form beyond that of the sons of men—
> so shall he startle many nations;
>> kings shall shut their mouths because of him;
> for that which has not been told them they shall see,
>> and that which they have not heard they shall understand.
>>> [Isa. 52:13-15]

> The Lord has bared his holy arm
>> before the eyes of all the nations;
> and all the ends of the earth shall see
>> the salvation of our God.
>>> [Isa. 52:10]

In Israel God has made history. In righteousness he judges his people and in mercy he redeems them. This has been the service of his people—to bear upon themselves the stripes of God's healing, the discipline of his divine purpose for their wholeness, their integrity, and that of the entire world (53:5). The eyes of the world will turn to gaze upon that which does not attract, the unattractive, the poor, the lowly, the humbled servant of God, who has no comeliness and no beauty (53:2). The rejected servant of God will teach the world of his ways with men. He will instruct the nations in what justice means, but not by lecturing or preaching, nor by setting himself up as a judge who imparts justice by accusation and sentence; still he will not fail or be discouraged until justice is established in the earth (42:1-4). This is the passive mission of Israel, to bear the judgment, and out of that judgment the salvation of God for the world to see.

> And he said to me, "You are my servant,
> Israel, in whom I will be glorified."
> [Isa. 49:3]

The purpose of the service of this servant is twofold. The servant figure is clearly the people Israel, as the text unmistakably says. However, as is equally clear in the text, one of the tasks of the servant is to effect the regathering or repentance of Israel to God (49:5). The difficulty that stems from these two verses has seemed insurmountable to many modern and ancient students of the prophet. How can the servant be Israel if part of the task of the servant is to bring Israel back to God? Many answers have been offered all the way from those based on textual emendation to those which view the servant either as an individual, like the patriarch Jacob, called Israel, or as a group within the nation Israel. The difficulty was noted already by those who heard the prophet himself speak twenty-five hundred years ago. Someone pointedly asked him how such a thing could be. The prophet's answer to the question was what is now the following verse:

> It is too light a thing that you should be my servant
>   to raise up the tribes of Jacob
>   and to restore the preserved of Israel;
> I will give you as a light to the nations,
>   that my salvation may reach to the end of the earth.
>   [Isa. 49:6]

The return of Israel to God will be effected in Israel's mission to the world. Israel will be regathered and restored unto God in the working out of her service as his servant.[7] This suggestion is oversimple, but it is thoroughly in line with the prophet's own thought; and it is thoroughly biblical. For instance, the earlier Isaiah had told King Ahaz, "If you do not have faith, you will surely not be established" [Isa. 7:9]. We have already noted other similar ideas in the message of the eighth-century Isaiah. And, of course, the New Testament is full of the idea that what God gives we most receive when we give it away; getting by losing is a biblical idea. And that is what our prophet is here saying: it is too light a thing that Israel should work only for her own restoration; on the contrary, only in giving herself as a light to the nations will Israel once again be Israel.

The prophet expresses the idea again in what I am sure should be regarded as the climax of his message. Those who gathered the sayings of the prophet and edited them correctly put the prophet's most exalted idea at the end of the collection, chapter 55. He here proclaims that God's redemption is free. All the Jews in exile may join in the procession, the poetically glorious return home across the desert. It is freely offered (52:3-6).

Ho, every one who thirsts,
    come to the waters;
and he who has no money,
    come, buy and eat!
Come, buy wine and milk
    without money and without price.
Why do you spend your money for that which is not bread,
    and your labor for that which does not satisfy?
                                                    [Isa. 55:1-2a]

Israel, all Israel collectively, has suffered double for her sins (40:2). All that she needs now do is come and accept the gracious gift of God.

Hearken diligently to me . . .
Incline your ear, and come to me . . .
and I will make with you an everlasting covenant . . .

like the covenant with David (55:2, 3). Just as David was a witness and a leader and commander among the peoples or tribes of Israel (55:4) so Israel will now be such among the nations of the world.

Behold, you shall call nations that you know not,
    and nations that knew you not shall run to you,
because of the Lord your God, and of the Holy One of Israel,
    for he has glorified you.

                                                    [Isa. 55:5]

It is no longer a case then of a covenant within Israel for Israel; just as Jeremiah hoped for a new covenant wherein the prophetic movement within Israel would be displaced by the larger concept of a prophetic Israel within the world, so this prophet proposes the same expansive concept of the mission of Israel based on the royal covenant. Israel will be as a king among nations calling and receiving the other nations of the world to impart to them knowledge of God. Just as the principal role of the king in Israel was that of supreme judge in the land representing and administering the will of God, so Israel is here viewed as the one among the nations of the world to impart to the world knowledge of the righteousness of God.

> . . . By his knowledge shall the righteous one, my servant,
> make many to be accounted righteous.
>
> [Isa. 53:11]

The mission of Israel is to "establish justice in the earth" (Isa. 42:4). Such is the new role of Israel, sometimes seen as a prophetic figure, sometimes as a royal figure. In her new role Israel exports a knowledge of God, the one true universal God, the judge and redeemer of Israel from old. Israel has grown up from her first inception as a nation under the call of God (49:1; 53:2). Israel has been taught and disciplined of God through judgment (49:2; 53:3) for the purpose of her mission (49:6; 53:4-6, 11). The Second Isaiah combines the figures of the prophet and king with that of witness throughout his message; for Israel will not just preach or proclaim and judge, she bears in herself the stripes of his judgment for the salvation of the world (53:5-6) and for the world to see.

The nations of the world will come to Israel because of the Lord, God (55:5). They will come not because Israel has material goods to trade, as nations trade with other nations for commerce. They will come for the sole purpose of learning of God. Israel must give away what she has to

the rest of the world. That which God has freely given her
(55:1) the nations will come to receive at her hand (55:5).
It is in this receiving and giving that Israel will be Israel.
It is in Israel's losing herself in service to God that she will
be restored to God, that she will find herself (49:6). The
great hope of our prophet is that this will really mean all
Israel. Hence, he issues a final call to all the Jews in exile
to come to the Lord at this great moment of salvation. Even
the wicked and the unrighteous have but to abandon their
apostasy and seek the Lord to receive this salvation and join
this new exodus, this going home.

> Seek the Lord while he may be found,
>   call ye upon him while he is near;
> let the wicked forsake his way,
>   and the unrighteous man his thoughts;
> let him return to the Lord, that he may have mercy on him,
>   and to our God, for he will abundantly pardon.
>
> [55:6-7]

This is, of course, rank injustice by human standards. That
even those who have abandoned the way of the Lord may
now join in the great act of redemption along with those
who all along had remained faithful and true to God, perhaps suffering for their faithfulness, is totally unjust. Some
good Jew, who had remained faithful throughout the
indignities of imprisonment and even perhaps of persecution
(42:22; 51:7; Ps. 137:5-6), put the question to the prophet:
"Mr. Prophet, do you mean to say that these sinners and
infidels receive the same reward as those of us who did not
waver but have from the beginning been faithful and obedient?" It is approximately the same complaint the laborers
made to the householder who had hired them in early morn-
ing, referring to those whom he had hired late in the day,

"These last worked only one hour, and you have made them equal to us who have borne the burden of the day and the scorching heat" (Matt. 20:12). The New Testament emphasizes this seemingly unjust aspect of the grace of God. Jesus emphasized throughout his ministry God's grace toward sinners.[8]

Such a question as the disgruntled laborers asked and, if we are right, was asked by the disgruntled faithful of the Second Isaiah's time is quite understandable. And our prophet answered the question in much the same way the householder answered it (Matt. 20:13-15).

> For my thoughts are not your thoughts,
>   neither are your ways my ways, says the Lord.
> For as the heavens are higher than the earth,
>   so are my ways higher than your ways
>   and my thoughts than your thoughts.
>   [Isa. 55:8-9]

Such is the grace of God that it is freely offered even to sinners.[9] Of course, such an idea as the prophet expounds must not be confused with the later idea of absolute grace. Here we clearly see that the apostate Jew, the wicked and the unrighteous, must forsake his ways and thoughts and return to the Lord to receive God's free gift of salvation, just as the laborers in the New Testament parable cited worked at least the one hour.

The principal point of the passage, however, is the prophet's proclamation that God is near, that he can now be found. This is the hour of redemption and salvation. This is the hour of theophany, or the moment of God's appearing. The "gospel" aspect of the Second Isaiah's message is to be seen in the glorious symphony to which we earlier referred. There all nature, all creation, seems to sense this saving act of God and offer accompaniment to the apostrophe, "Behold your God!" (Isa. 40:9). The complement to that proclamation is in another movement to the same symphonic chorus:

> How beautiful upon the mountains
>   are the feet of him who brings good tidings,
> who publishes peace, who brings good tidings of good,
>   who publishes salvation,
>   who says to Zion, "Your God reigns."
>
> [Isa. 52:7]

The good news is the sovereignty of God. It was the same message the earlier prophets proclaimed. They emphasized judgment and looked forward, most of them, to the salvation that would issue from it. The Second Isaiah emphasized salvation and constantly insisted that it issued from the prior judgment. For them all, however, it is essentially the same message—that of the universal, inevitable, inescapable lordship, kingship, and sovereignty of God, who rules his people with an everlasting love.

CHAPTER VI

IT IS FINISHED

The same sovereignty of God is effective both for judgment and for salvation. Moreover, God as sovereign ruler never ceases to judge those whom he loves. "God judges" means "God rules." "For the Lord is our judge, the Lord is our ruler, the Lord is our King; he will save us" (Isa. 33:22). But in that very judgment, that very sovereignty, is our salvation. Outside it there is no salvation. The basic lesson of the Book of Job at its simplest level is that God judges even our righteousness, our goodness, our obedience, and our innocence. We have not bought God off by obeying him. We cannot escape his terrible love (Amos 5:18-19; Ps. 139:1-12; Rom. 8:35-39). God comes to us, all the way. There is no escape in all creation, in all the created order, from his sovereign power and love. The only thing finally to be said is that the closer we are to him the more powerful is his presence and his rule.

The New Testament emphasizes the judgment of God in a manner even harsher than does the Old Testament. The New Testament turns around the Old Testament insistence, that judgment is salvation, and proclaims that even God's grace is really his judgment over us. In Paul's words, grace makes us slaves of righteousness (Rom. 6:18). We are in no sense free of the righteous sovereignty of God when we have accepted grace and confess that it is God's righteousness, and not our own, which saves us. Humbly to confess that we cannot save ourselves but that only by the righteousness of God are we saved, is the judgment of grace in New Testament terms.

The cross for the church signifies at one and the same time that judgment and that grace. And it is a harsher, crueler judgment than anything we have seen in the Old Testament. The cross constantly reminds us that God comes to us even in our rejection of him. It constantly says to us that God reaches out to us even in the worst thing mankind can do or has ever done, the rejection of the grace itself. Though we crucified him when he came to us in Christ, God speaks to us still, even in that crucifixion: I do love you still. There is the "no escape." We rejected him; we killed him. And in the rejection and in the killing he comes to us. Nothing can separate us from the love of God, the awe-ful, terrible love of God. And somehow we realize that this judgment is harsher and crueler than if, as upon Israel, he would but pour his wrath upon us. No, he comes to us when we reject him and says from the cross, I do love you still. The judgment and the salvation, the curse and the grace, are one. The cross accuses us and forgives us. It judges us and redeems us.

In the manner of the worship life of ancient Israel let us now look at ourselves in the mirror of the passion account. Let us take two phrases, one from Paul in I Corinthians 11:23, and one from the fourth evangelist in John 19:30. In the one we see ourselves, as the church, live through the long night which preceded the day of the crucifixion. And in the other we see ourselves, as the world, endure a moment it has never really escaped.

One of the outstanding factors in the cultic rites of Old Testament Israel was the act of remembrance, which we call today *anamnesis*.[2] By this cultic principle Israel saw herself reflected in the stories which made up her cultic, or holy, history. For instance, by this principle later Israel claimed for herself in each generation the experience of the Exodus, or the vicissitudes and victories of Abraham and Jacob. Thus there was the sense of corporate personality whereby the patriarch Jacob was Israel latent or the people Israel were Jacob patent. The pattern of the interpersonal tensions between Jacob and Esau was the pattern of inter-tribal and international relations between Israel and Edom, or other nations. The blessings of Jacob (Gen. 49) or of Moses (Deut. 33) upon the twelve patriarchs became little mirrors wherein the later tribes saw themselves well reflected. By the same principle, the church finds itself reflected in the gospel story. It is remarkable how the vicissitudes and victories of the twelve disciples are a portrait of the church since that time.

"In the same night that he was betrayed he took bread. . ." (I Cor. 11:23). These are words with which we are too familiar. We have repeated them and heard them so often that they have become but a verbal accompaniment to the celebration of the Holy Communion. They are like a cue line from a prompter. We don't think of their meaning, we but use them to get started with the periodic little drama we perform as a part of the church program.

Even when we do think of their meaning it is usually in terms of a proper exegesis which includes dealing with the exact date of the crucifixion. Which night? Passover eve

or the night before? Or we think, rightly, of the persistence
of the Bible in giving date lines to what it offers as divine
revelation.

We should think more primitively and radically about
Paul's tradition on the timing of this meal. The relevancy
of the timing for us is sufficiently expressed in the temporal
clause, "In the same night that he was betrayed. . . ." For
you see, that was our night, our big moment to be all that
we should have been. We live that night through again and
again. We know it well. And the remarkable thing is that
there is nothing particularly wrong with how we live that
night. Everything we do all that night long is normal and
understandable—until the force of the next phrase strikes
us, ". . . he took bread. . . ." And then somehow we can't
quite bear ourselves. Our excuses and defenses and deceits
are shattered. The defensible and normal become offensive
and shameful. He took bread on the same night that he was
betrayed.

That was our night, the night the church was conceived.
And we were all there, all twelve of us, seated about the
table. The more we study the scene in the Upper Room the
more we realize that in those twelve men the church is
accurately portrayed. But—and this is the frightful thing—
the more we study each disciple, his words and his actions,
and the whole group in their words and actions, the more
we know that each of us and all of us were there, singly
and collectively. We come to realize that what they said and
did is precisely what we would have said and done; that
what they said and did is exactly what we say and do.

Let us, therefore, reassemble in the Upper Room both to
sit about the table and to look at ourselves, all twelve of
us. It will be traumatic and if we are not ready to see our-

selves as we are, then we should not come. For to shy from seeing ourselves as we really are is to confess that we have no place about that table: we deny that we are a part of that conception; we admit that we have not been born into the church.

Let us return in historic memory to our place about the table (Luke 22).* *Then Satan entered into Judas Iscariot, who was of the number of the twelve.* The shock is too much. Why must we look first at Judas? Yet we know that because Judas was there we are not excluded. And we thank God that he was at the table when our Lord took bread and broke it. What if he had not been? Then that bread would not be for me. I, Judas the betrayer, am at the table and receive the bread and the cup. If he had excluded me then I would have known for certain that I had done right in selling out. But no, there it is, the bread from his own hand he bids me eat. In the same night that I betrayed him he took bread and blessed it and broke it and gave it to me.

But we don't know who it is our Lord means when he says that the betrayer is at the table with him. So, the text says, *we began to wonder who it was that would do such a thing.* And then the most normal thing happened; we all started bickering. Normal, because when we protest our innocence we trot out our record of good deeds. How could it be I? I was with him in Galilee, at Caesarea Philippi, I went out with the seventy, etc. So, we started the bickering about who would be the greatest in the kingdom. Look at my record, we say. We forget the word of judgment and start our bickering. The picture of the church grows clearer. And we don't stop our bickering until our Lord assures us

* Words quoted from the passion accounts in the Gospels appear in italic type throughout the remainder of this chapter.

that each of us will have a throne and be a servant.

And then he turns to Peter and says to us, "Simon, Satan wants you *but I have prayed for you.* You will deny me this night, all night you will deny that you know me—right up to dawn itself." And he looks deep into our eyes as he will later on from the balcony and we make our feeble vows of fidelity. "To prison and to death I'll go—but not tonight."

Then knowing the stuff we're made of he tells us to bring our moneybags and our swords and accompany him to the garden. Oh, how he knows us better than we ever know ourselves. We must have our money and our swords; for these are our crutches; these are our ego. These protect us from ourselves. They build our ego and we need them lest we face the awful truth of who we are.

But we don't use them for a while yet. We go into the garden and he bids us watch and pray while he goes off alone himself to pray. He asks us to be men for him as he goes himself into the totality of loneliness to experience the agony himself of being a man. *Remove this cup from me* and he perspired drops of blood. If there is a blood atonement this is it: Jesus experiencing the agony of being a man, fully and completely and totally. I am a man; oh God, I don't seek suffering and death; I don't want to die.

His loneliness is but accentuated when he returns to find us asleep. He asked us to be men for him a man and we fall asleep. The picture of the church becomes clearer.

And then it happened. The soldiers and the priests and Judas came. And Judas kissed him. Then our ire up, our indignation kindled, we rise to the occasion. *Lord, shall we strike with the sword?* And one of us strikes a slave of the high priest and cuts off his ear. We wake up from our lethargy; indignant and self-righteous we gather our forces, we muster our strength to go forth to the fray and we nick a little piece of an ear. What awful reality is this in the passion account when we see ourselves for what we are. Jesus says to the crowd, *This is your hour*. And we all flee, every one of us abandons him with our purses and our swords.

But this is the church's night, the same night that he broke bread. Then Peter. With Peter we deny we ever knew him. All our feeble vows are of no avail. We never knew him.

And then with the rays of dawn he looks at us from the balcony. *The Lord turned and looked at Peter*. And with Peter we go out and weep bitterly.

And that was the same night that he broke bread with us. But the picture means nothing until we accept that bread and that cup. For we have no place in the picture unless we accept him. He offers himself through the din of our bertayals and bickering and feeble vows and lethargy and folly and denials. Through it all his hand proffers the broken bread. Take, eat, broken for you. In the same night that he was betrayed he took bread—and begot us, the church.

When Jesus had received the vinegar, he said, "It is finished"; and he bowed his head and gave up his spirit (John 19:30).

What does it mean, this word *tetelestai—It is finished?* According to John it accompanies the very expiration of Jesus' last breath. What does it mean? There are so many possibilities.

The form critics are probably right in seeing the so-called "last seven words" as later accretions. If we are interested in what really happened we must probably be satisfied with the likelihood of a simple outcry of pain and anguish. What the evangelists are trying to say, as so often elsewhere in the Gospels, is that the crucifixion fits into the divine pattern. The point that had first to be established for the faith and mission of the church was that this crucifixion was not just another that Josephus might chronicle alongside that of the eight hundred Pharisees whom Alexander Jannaeus crucified in 88 B.C., or those crucified in the War of Varus in 4 B.C. This was no accident of history.

In other words, the crucifixion is not ultimately what it seems to be, a tragedy of life, another case of a good man unjustly accused—a miscarriage of human justice. Far from that, it is the true statement of divine judgment on all mankind. Yet at the same time it is the true statement of divine grace. God did not conquer sin and solve man's predicament by fighting evil with evil but by conquering evil with suffering love. Simply put, the evangelists wanted simply to say: This is not only a fact of history; this is the true sovereignty of God.

Then what is meant by *tetelestai—It is finished?* From the days of slavery we inherit the spiritual, "Were you there when they crucified my Lord?" Let us look carefully into the mirror which the last moments of Jesus' life affords, to see if perhaps the world has ever really escaped that moment or if in some sense we must not hear for ourselves the anguished cry, "It is finished."

Suppose we gather about the cross and observe the reactions of those the passion account tells us heard or might have heard this fearsome cry. We are told in Matthew that at Jesus' final word the curtain of the temple was torn in two and in the Gospel to the Hebrews that a large lintel of the temple fell down. Nature's response to this divine judgment was, as in the prophets, in concert with the curse, a fall of darkness at midday. Nature's response was, therefore, in the early Christian cultus clear and sharp. What was man's response? What meaning did it have, this awesome cry, to those present, those who were there when they crucified my Lord?

There were the two thieves, the one desperate for his life whose last hope of clinging to an empty existence was this teacher, this man of whom he had heard as the Christ. *Save yourself and us!* Let's see you make good your claims. Like the tempter in the desert at the start of Jesus' career, this man at the end of his life challenged Jesus to show his supernatural powers. But all Jesus could respond was *It is finished.* Disappointment and derision were the reaction of the first thief—Yeah, it's over, but good. I knew you couldn't do anything for anybody, anyway. You're a big joke, Jesus. All life's one big joke. And we hear his raucous, derisive, but frightened laughter pierce our own doubting hearts.

There was the second thief, and the centurion. Their reaction was much the same. *We are receiving the due reward of our deeds; but this man has done nothing wrong* is the rebuke of the so-called "good thief" to his weak companion. Likewise the centurion, according to Luke, said *certainly this man was innocent.* These two statements represent at least the reactions of most men since that day. Jesus' crucifixion is history's prime example of the miscarriage of justice, the innocent oppressed and unjustly accused. This is humanism at its best: the cross is man's sin, his inability because of his own fears and insecurity, to insure justice's true balance and right execution, that trapped in his own fears and ambitions man yet fails to guarantee his own rights and dignity. *Certainly this man was innocent,* says the centurion, to our shame and to our failure.

Then there were the Roman soldiers. It was noon, they say, when they crucified him. Assigned to a detail they did their job. *And they crucified him.* A soldier doesn't ask why he drew this or that assignment; he does what he is ordered to do. *And they crucified him.* Nasty job to pull. But somebody has to. When your number's up, your number's up. *And they crucified him.* Wretched day. Hot. Humid. Cloudy. Storm brewing. Anybody for a quick game? *And they cast lots to divide his garments.* Thirsty! Listen to that one. He's thirsty! Who in Hades isn't on a damnable day like this? Here, give him some of that vinegar they throw out on their passover—that'll show him a thirst! If you are the king of the Jews, get out of this one—if you can! Not exactly a kingly brew, a royal potion. *Father, forgive them. It is finished.* A bad job; but it's over now. *It is finished.* Another day, another shekel.

Annas and Caiaphas heard it, and so did their legal advisers. A close call on that one. Seditious rebel. Can't afford to have the Romans on our necks for the likes of him. Jeopardize the whole nation? Not on his life! King of Israel indeed! But it's over now. Case of the traitor Jesus closed. *It is finished.*

The crowd dwindles. The shouting subsides. Wagging their heads they snort and chuckle. Destroy the temple! Who did he think he was? Rebuild it in three days! He fancied himself at playing Solomon. Good riddance, I say. That was a good one. But, *it is finished* now.

Somewhere in the shadows lurks a freed man. Released from prison, his first day out of jail. Barabbas delivered from bondage! Term of sentence finished.

Off in the distance on the palace balcony, stand Pilate and his wife. A nightmare come true, but after all—I didn't really know him. It wasn't as though he were somebody important. What's done's done. *What I have written I have written*, says he. Call the houseboy and have him remove this bowl and make sure he cleans the ring around the bowl. If there is anything I can't stand, says he, it's a dirty washbowl. The towel too. I like things neat and trim, nothing half done, you know. And that's that. *It is finished*.

Back in the shadows on the hill a few remain. The disciples and the women. The tragic end of a noble adventure. Everything seemed fine last night at supper. I gave up my fishing, my whole life, to follow him. And it comes to this. What went wrong? What happened? Nothing means anything anymore. You bet your life on the best you know, and then this. It's all over. All I've believed in, everything I've put my faith in. *It is finished*. Disillusionment. Disappointment. Tragedy. Return to Galilee and return to trying to make a living fishing. That's all there is now. *It is finished*.

Down the hill a way stands a husky fellow, a field laborer looking pensively at the figure on the cross. Simon of Cyrene says to himself, I thought it would help a bit to carry the cross. I didn't realize until now the harder part—to have the cross carry you. Just to hang there. Poor fellow. I guess he's glad *it is finished*. He had the rough part. Just hanging there. It's good it is all over now; a body just couldn't take much more. *It is finished*.

All kinds of people look for the Kingdom of God, like Joseph, the one from Arimathea. A pious man if ever there was one. A member of a local small town Sanhedrin. You can't blame him, though. He didn't have anything to do with this. He's against capital punishment in the first place, and not only that, he couldn't be sure about Jesus—he was looking for the Kingdom of God. But too late now. The finish it is.

But in the stillness of eternity did you ever hear a heart break? In the chill of infinity did you ever hear the heart of God break? *I have given the beloved of my soul into the hand of the enemy* (Jer. 12:7).

But *it is finished*. God broke his own heart and it was finished. The love of God pursued us every one to that hill where the cross stands. What does it mean to us that it is finished? Not with armies celestial or apocalyptic cataclysm, not with swords loud clashing, nor vengeance, nor rebuke, nor justice, nor just deserts: the strife is o'er, the battle done! *It is finished*. Love pursued sin and evil, corruption, ignorance, rebellion, and pride all the way to Calvary and nailed them to the cross. We have done our worst. Man can do no worse than he has already done. *It is finished*. No Enochian Son of Man appearing in the clouds with angelic armies won this battle. No, God just broke his heart. And *it is finished*.

The strife is o'er, the battle done; the victory of life is won;
The song of triumph has begun; *It is finished!*
The powers of death have done their worst, but Christ their legions has dispersed.
Let shouts of holy joy outburst; *It is finished!*

Then I looked, and I heard around the throne . . . the voice of many angels, and the number of them was ten thousand times ten thousand, and thousands of thousands, saying with a loud voice, "Worthy is the Lamb who was slain to receive power and riches and wisdom and might and honor and glory and blessing." And I heard every creature in heaven and on earth and under the earth and in the sea saying, "To him who sits upon the throne and to the Lamb be blessing and honor and glory and might forever and ever!" Amen.

[Rev. 5:11-14]

CHAPTER VII

TO THE GLORY OF GOD THE FATHER

The thrust of the gospel is God's quest for man, not man's search for God. The power of the gospel, its stumbling block, that which claims and traps and ensnares us, is not in the doctrine that Christ is or was divine, but in the biblical assertion that God entered his creation, "emptied himself, taking the form of a servant, being born in the likeness of men" (Phil. 2:7). The central problem of Christology is not that of Christ's divinity but rather that of God's humanity.[1] It is the manward thrust of God, not the Godward aspiration of man, that is the heart of the biblical story. Many cultures have advanced candidates for apotheosis. The New Testament, by contrast, presents to the world not one who attained divinity, but one in whom God chose to make himself known. "Men of Israel, hear these words: Jesus of Nazareth, a man attested to you by God with mighty works and wonders and signs which God did through him in your midst, as you yourselves know . . ." (Acts 2:22).

While it is quite true that the New Testament advances ideas about the Christ for which the Old Testament does not prepare us, it must, nonetheless, be unequivocally affirmed

that the root of the neotestamental Christologies (the New
Testament does not lack variety in such matters) is deeply
grounded in the Old Testament. The Old Testament is
canon to the New. In its argument that Jesus is the Christ,
the Lord and head of the church, which is itself the New
Israel, the New Testament knows no other criterion than
the Old. It accepts only the Old Testament as judge of
whether or not its claims are valid.[2] The New Testament
insists that a proper understanding of Christ must be derived from the Old Testament. It further affirms that all is
old, that in Christ the older order is fulfilled. Nothing here,
it wants to say, is innovation; all is old brought to fruition.[3]
The New Testament constantly presupposes the Old Testament. It assumes the faith which is there expressed.

There are objections which are rightly raised when such
statements as the foregoing are made. One is that close study
of the New Testament uses of Old Testament scripture
often betrays what modern scholarship would be forced to
call a misuse of the passages cited. We often wonder at what
must be called sheer misunderstanding on the part of the
New Testament writer. He often seems to be interested
only in a word here or there that suits his purpose. And
quite often he reads a meaning into the Old Testament
passage which it never had.

Two things must be said. The first is that we are wrong,
in our scholarly attitudes, to expect the New Testament
writer merely to rehash his Old Testament text. In order
to accept the New Testament on its own ground we must
permit it its understanding not only of the Old Testament,
but also of the sovereignty and providence of God in *its*
time. For the purpose of the New Testament was not
primarily to exposit scripture. The purpose of the early

church was to proclaim to the world a new thing, nay, the new and perfect act of God, in *its* time. When then it came to argue its position and to present the message to various and sundry peoples from differing backgrounds, the church enthusiastically set about to show the world how this last act of God was in line with what he had done in and through Israel, was, indeed, the culmination of all his work, the fulfillment of the whole history and story of what God had done as told in the scriptures, the law, the prophets, and psalms (Luke 24:44). It was an argument which combined the forces of appeal to antiquity and modernity. What it had to tell was of an event which had just transpired; but it was an event which could be seen evolving out of the purposes, the love and the justice, the power and the mercy, of the God whom Israel knew. No novelty, this! No passing fancy. Therefore, we must remind ourselves that the *raison d'être* of the New Testament gospel was the telling abroad of how God had just done this thing, this wonderful heart-rending thing, for all mankind. The New Testament was not written, as were the contemporary tannaitic and later rabbinical *midrashim*, primarily as exposition of scripture to show its timely relevance. Exposition of the Old Testament in the New has a purpose which transcends its use, the proclamation of the new work of God, in Christ.

The other thing which must be said is that when New Testament hermeneutics of Old Testament exegesis are compared to those in contemporary Judaism, and particularly to those used in Qumran, as evidenced in the so-called Dead Sea Scrolls, we are struck by the sense of Old Testament history which the New Testament writers exhibit.[4] The matter is not so serious as we might have thought had we only the New Testament from the period to judge by.

Another objection which might be raised, to the above-stated assertion that the New Testament accepts only the Old Testament as canon or criterion or judge of its claim for Christ and the church, is that such a position, usually voiced by Old Testament students, ignores the contemporary Hellenistic mentality and make-up of the New Testament. It ill behooves the Old Testament specialist, for all his enthusiasm about the relevance of the testaments, to ignore, or worse, to be ignorant of the variety of strands of thinking that go to form the complex New Testament image of the Christ.

One of the current debates among New Testament scholars centers in the question of how much, if any, gnosticism is in the New Testament. Part of the debate stems from work being done on the so-called Nag-Hammadi texts discovered in 1945 in Egypt, the Gospel of Thomas, and others being published or soon to be published.[5] Whatever gnosticism is there it cannot, certainly, be traced to the Old Testament. One of the great points of the current debate revolves around the question of whether a gnostic savior-redeemer myth is reflected in the New Testament idea of the pre-existence of Christ (Phil. 2:6; Col. 1:15-20; I Tim. 3:16).[6]

Such are the problems concerning which the Old Testament specialist can but offer sympathetic encouragement to his New Testament colleagues. And it ill becomes him either to ignore such problems or to belittle them.

Granting all that, there is an aspect of the question of the Old Testament in the New to which the Old Testament student feels impelled, nay, forced to address himself with enthusiasm. Perhaps those of us who do not know all the minute problems the New Testament raises, can offer, in our innocence, a perspective. To go *from* the Old Testament *to* the New is correct. It is natural; it is right. This is not because when we get there we feel we are already acquainted with what the New Testament has to say, or because we feel the evangelists or Paul have "correctly" quoted and used the prophets and psalmists. For all their inaccuracies they have used the Old Testament forcefully in their own way and for their purpose. And they certainly use it as "correctly" as do their contemporaries, the rabbis and the sectarians.

But all that is not the point. The point is that what the New Testament says, not in all particulars about Christ, but about God, is what the Old Testament says about God. There we do meet again the creator-transcendant God of the priestly school. There we do meet again the provident-sustaining God of the Yahwist and Elohist. There we do meet the loving, judging-redeeming God of the prophets. There we see at work Amos' and Isaiah's and Jeremiah's God. If anything, we seem to see him more clearly in his Christ than we do in his Israel. What Abraham and Moses and Hosea and Jeremiah tell us about him seems to take shape in this Christ—this Christ who judges us to the quick, and quickens us by his love. It is as though he judges us from afar in the Old Testament while here he smites our hearts so that there is no escaping the love with which he does it.

In the Old Testament we find the recurring theme: Judgment is salvation. In the New the theme finds us, each of us where he stands. Two things seem to have happened. God's reach, in Christ, has become both universal and personal. The Isaiah of the Exile had indicated how universal God's reach was, and Jeremiah had shown how personal it could be. And here, in Christ, the two are joined. "Jesus Christ is the universal judge because he is the universal savior."[7] There is no salvation outside this being caught and trapped by God, this being indicted by his love. "Wherever Christ goes he brings both judgment and salvation."[8] The salvation is in the judgment.

And somehow, in going from the Old to the New Testament, our expectations are fulfilled. The Old Testament makes us wish we had been in Israel, an Israelite, to know, as the prophets and the others knew, the intimate fellowship of the God who had known their sufferings and who had judged them because they were his. Then we step into the New and there before the cross we fall on our face, taken and claimed. The God in whose council Jeremiah had stood (Jer. 23:22), invites us all into his presence, everybody personally. He has come all the way; for here, in the cross, he has overcome the final barrier: he has come even in our rejection of him. And so, when Paul says he "emptied himself" and "humbled himself" (Phil. 2:7-8) we know, as never before, the sovereignty of God. He "did not count equality with God a thing to be grasped" (2:6). That is the sovereignty of God, yes, and the majesty and the power which only the one eternal God has, that he need not grasp it. Only God himself, one and unique, majestic, sovereign, and transcendant, can do that.

The question of the divinity of Christ seems now irrelevant. For what we now see is God, who so loved his creation that he pleased himself to take on the form of a servant. If in Christ we Christians do not see the work of God we are idolaters and sinners in the highest degree. Christ is Christ because he is transparent, because in him we see

God's work, nothing less. Christ is Christ because he pretends nothing for himself. In the highest sense Christ reveals God and it is God who acts in Christ. "Therefore God has highly exalted him . . . to the glory of God the Father" (Phil. 2:9-11). As in the Old Testament God is still the subject of the verbs! If Christ is Lord it is because God worked in him and made him so. We do not, we must not, worship Christ. Apart from the God of Abraham, Moses, Amos, Isaiah, and Jeremiah there is no Christ. We worship God who came to us in Christ and comes to us through his Holy Spirit—all the way. There must never be the least mitigation of the monotheism of the Trinity.

In Christ God judges us at our best. The power of the gospel strikes us, not in our "total depravity," but in our best efforts to be responsible, obedient, good, and decent. Paul has a harsh expression to the point. "For God has consigned all men to disobedience that he may have mercy upon all" (Rom. 11:32). When we approach the cross we know what he meant and we know he is right. Judas' worst fault was that he took the advice of the church leaders, the priests of his day, and for services rendered received an honorarium. The church leaders' worst fault was an effort to save the church and state of their day from political and perhaps physical disaster at the hands of the Romans. Peter's worst fault, in his denying his Lord, was that he had followed him to his trial, whereas the others had not. Pilate's worst fault was in abstaining from making a decision he rightly felt incompetent to make. The Roman soldiers' worst fault was in their obedience to the orders to which they were assigned. And in them all we see ourselves, and we know that we too put him there. Is it depravity to follow the advice of our priests and bishops? Is it depravity for priests and bishops to try to save church and state from disaster? Is it depravity to follow our Lord in his trials though we cannot join him on the cross? Is it wrong to abstain from judgment? Is it wrong to be obedient? Each of us knows experientially and personally the life situation of those who crucified our Lord.

> Who was the guilty? Who brought this upon thee?
>   Alas, my treason, Jesus, hath undone thee!
> 'Twas I, Lord Jesus, I it was denied thee:
>   I crucified thee.[9]

Like them we have our own excuses, our own special circumstances, which we plead in defense. But then we are confronted by the cross.

> See, from his head, his hands, his feet,
>   Sorrow and love flow mingled down.
> Did e'er such love and sorrow meet,
>   Or thorns compose so rich a crown?[10]

And we know that our excuses are nothing. The brief wherewith we would defend ourselves crumbles like dust in our pleading hands. We see all our goodness and our righteousness shattered in the shocking sight before us.

> We have all become like one who is unclean,
>   And all our righteous deeds are like a filthy rag.
>   [Isa. 64:6a]

No excuse or defense we can proffer could increase the love which there surrounds us or the forgiveness which there indicts us. And then we realize that salvation is also judgment, a judgment harsher and crueler than any of which the Old Testament speaks, the judgment of his grace: I do love you still.

NOTES

Introduction

1. See the writer's "Habakkuk in Qumran, Paul and the Old Testament," *The Journal of Religion*, Vol. XXXIX, 1959, pp. 232-44, wherein such views are refuted.

Chapter I. *The Christian Story*

1. This, however, does not mean that the Christian denies general revelation, God's speaking through nature and general history. Here we are concerned with the biblical personal God, who reveals himself in the particular story of Israel and Christ. See E. C. Blackman's excellent discussion of particular and general revelation in his *Biblical Interpretation*, 1957, pp. 30-31.

2. Bonhoeffer, *Prisoner for God*, 1953, pp. 142-43.

3. See G. Ernest Wright, *The Old Testament Against Its Environment*, 1950, pp. 20-29. There are exceptions in the Bible which but prove the rule, notably I Kings 22 and Job 1.

4. See the excellent article by James Barr, "The Meaning of 'Mythology' in Relation to the Old Testament," *Vetus Testamentum*, Vol. IX, 1959, pp. 1-10; see also the incisive treatise by Brevard Childs, *Myth and Reality in the Old Testament*, 1960.

5. An amplification of the list in Gerhard von Rad's "Das formgeschichtliche Problem des Hexateuch" in *Gesammelte Studien zum Alten Testament*, 1958, pp. 11-20.

6. Robinson, *The History of Israel*, 1938, pp. 232-33, 239.

7. I am gratefully indebted for this idea to my colleague, Prof. H. R. Holcomb.

8. See also Josh. 24:2-13; Neh. 9:1-37; Dan. 9:4-19.

9. Mic. 6:4-5; Hos. 9:10, 11:1-4, 12:9-13, 13:4-5; Isa. 5:1-7; Jer. 2:2-8, 7:21-26; Ezek. 16 and 20.

Chapter II. *Creation and the Creator*

1. G. Ernest Wright, *Biblical Archaeology*, 1958, pp. 102-3, 118-19.

2. William Neil, *The Rediscovery of the Bible*, 1954, pp. 29-42. E. C. Blackman, *Biblical Interpretation*, 1957, pp. 9-22.

3. See the excellent discussion of Ps. 19 by Henri Frankfort, in Frankfort *et al.*, *The Intellectual Adventure of Ancient Man*, p. 363. Frankfort's suggestion that the psalmist was really mocking the beliefs of Egyptians and Babylonians has given the writer the courage to see satirical overtones in Gen. 1. Also see Ludwig Köhler's *Old Testament Theology*, 1957, pp. 88, for a perceptive view of the eschatological importance of Gen. 1.

4. Paul Humbert in *Opuscules d'un hébraïsant*, 1958, p. 153, sees *bara'* as similar in meaning, in Gen. 1, to *'asah*.

5. Note that man made in God's image is directly in contrast to idols made in the image of men and animals. See *Vita Adae et Evae*, XIII-XV, where angels are commanded by God to worship his image in man (Charles, *Apocrypha and Pseudepigrapha*, II, p. 137).

6. See Meredith G. Kline's "Because It Had Not Rained," *Westminster Theological Journal*, Vol. 20, 1958, pp. 146-57.

7. See Abraham Heschel's sensitive treatment of the idea of the sanctification of time, not space, as heralded at creation (Gen. 2:3; Exod. 20:8, 11) by God's blessing the Sabbath and making it holy, in *The Sabbath*, 1951, pp. 8-10.

8. See Wright, *The Old Testament Against Its Environment*, pp. 30-41, and his article in *The Interpreter's Bible*, Vol. I, especially p. 361.

9. See Cuthbert Simpson's discussion of the problem in *The Interpreter's Bible*, Vol. I, p. 450. See also Skinner in the *Inter-*

national Critical Commentary, Vol. I, pp. 41-47, and Wright in *Biblical Archaeology*, 1958, pp. 118-19.

10. See, for example, such apocryphal works as *The Epistle of Jeremy* and *Wisdom of Solomon.*

11. James B. Pritchard, ed., *Ancient Near Eastern Texts Related to the Old Testament*, 1950, pp. 60-61.

12. Cf. Jer. 4:23 and Isa. 34:11, and see Hermann Gunkel, *Genesis*, 1910, p. 103.

13. Cf. Skinner, *op. cit.*, p. 20.

14. See also Price, *et al.*, *The Monuments and the Old Testament*, 1958, pp. 100-127.

15. See the references to ancient literature on this point in Gunkel, *op. cit.*, p. 104.

16. See Louis F. Hartman's "Sin in Paradise," *Catholic Biblical Quarterly*, Vol. 20, 1958, pp. 26-40, where it is suggested that in Gen. 3 the tree, the fruit, and the serpent have sexual connotations and that the sin involved was nature worship. Hartman has seen in Gen. 3 what is here suggested in Gen. 1.

17. Gunkel, *op. cit.*, p. 101, wrongly puts this phrase before Gen. 1:1.

18. Wright and Fuller, *The Book of the Acts of God*, 1957, p. 30.

19. Robinson, *The Cross in the Old Testament*, 1955, p. 47.

Chapter IV. *Judgment and Salvation*

1. See the excellent treatise of George Mendenhall, *Law and Covenant in Israel and the Ancient Near East*, The Biblical Colloquium, 1955, reprinted from *The Biblical Archaeologist*, Vol. XVII, 1954, pp. 26-46 and 49-76.

2. For a fuller development of the meaning of these and similar passages, see the writer's *Suffering as Divine Discipline*, Colgate Rochester Divinity School *Bulletin*, special issue, 1955.

3. The preceding verse, 31:4 (cf. 10:12), makes it clear that Isaiah has not changed his mind about the extent of God's judgment; it is a complete judgment for the redemption of city and temple.

4. The debate continues as to whether Gomer was a harlot,

even a cultic prostitute, when Hosea married her. See H. H. Rowley, "The Marriage of Hosea," *Bulletin of the John Rylands Library*, Vol. 39, 1956-57, pp. 200-33. If, however, the analogy the prophet himself makes is valid, then the early marriage relationship of Hosea and Gomer was a wholesome one.

Chapter V. *Judgment and Salvation* continued

1. Literally: "But from it he will be saved." However, the Hebrew permits of the idea contained in the translation offered, which is the idea Jeremiah elsewhere more clearly states. See the writer's *Suffering as Divine Discipline*, p. 62.

2. For the meaning of *ḥesed* and a defense of this translation, see the writer's *Suffering as Divine Discipline*, p. 63.

3. *Ibid.*, pp. 74-78.

4. On this point of apostasy in exile see the writer's "Thy God Reigneth," *motive*, February, 1956.

5. See S. H. Blank's "Studies in Deutero-Isaiah," *Hebrew Union College Annual*, Vol. XV, 1940, pp. 1-46, and Julian Morgenstern's "Deutero-Isaiah's Terminology for 'Universal God,'" *Journal of Biblical Literature*, Vol. LXII, 1943, pp. 269-80.

6. See the writer's *Suffering as Divine Discipline*, pp. 97-100.

7. See *Ibid.*, pp. 99-100, for the references and argument necessary to the point; see also his article already referred to in *motive*, February, 1956, p. 31.

8. See Joachim Jeremias, "The Qumran Texts and the New Testament," *Expository Times*, December, 1958, pp. 68-69.

9. It is possible that the figure of the rain and snow which immediately follows in Isa. 55:10-11 may be compared to the saying of Jesus in Matt. 5:45.

Chapter VI. *It Is Finished*

1. The hebraist needs but reflect on the basic meaning and connotations of the verb *shaphaṭ* and the noun *mishpaṭ*.

2. See Aage Bentzen, *King and Messiah*, 1955, pp. 11-12, and

the reference on p. 83, in note 6, to N. A. Dahl, "Anamnesis," *Studia Theologica*, I, 1-2, 1947, pp. 69 ff.; cf. Joachim Jeremias, *The Eucharistic Words of Jesus*, 1955, and Marjorie H. Sykes, "The Eucharist as 'Anamnesis,'" *Expository Times*, January, 1960, pp. 115-18.

Chapter VII. *To the Glory of God the Father*

1. Note the title of the recent book, *The Humanity of God*, 1960, a collection of three essays by Karl Barth, and see especially pp. 37-65.

2. See the writer's "Habakkuk in Qumran, Paul and the Old Testament," *The Journal of Religion*, Vol. XXXIX, 1959, pp. 232-44, where the pertinent arguments are set forth.

3. See the incisive comments to the point by Krister Stendahl, *The Scrolls and the New Testament*, 1957, pp. 1-17.

4. Cf. F. F. Bruce, *Biblical Exegesis in the Qumran Texts*, 1959, p. 71.

5. For a bibliography complete to date, cf. Søren Giverson, "Bibliography on the Nag-Hammadi Manuscripts," *Acta Orientalia*, Vol. XXIV, 3-4, 1959, pp. 189-98. For additional references cf. Robert M. Grant, "Two Gnostic Gospels," *Journal of Biblical Literature*, Vol. LXXIX, 1960, pp. 1-11.

6. Kurt Schubert, in *Die Gemeinde vom Toten Meer*, 1958, pp. 62-69, contends that there was pre-Christian gnosticism in apocalyptic Judaism. The writer remains unconvinced. On the notion of pre-existence in pre-Christian Judaism, however, it must be remembered that in *Jubilees* torah is pre-existent and in the *Assumption of Moses* (1:4; 3:12) Moses himself is pre-existent.

7. Joseph Huby, *Saint Paul, Épître aux Romains*, 1957, p. 119.

8. Sherman Johnson, "The Preaching to the Dead," *Journal of Biblical Literature*, Vol. LXXIX, 1960, p. 51.

9. Johann Heermann, *ca.* 1630.

10. Isaac Watts, 1707.

INDEX OF NAMES AND SUBJECTS

Terms which express the general theme of the book and appear very frequently, such as sovereignty, love, grace, judgment, salvation, and redemption, are not listed in the index.

INDEX OF SCRIPTURE QUOTATIONS

*Chapter and verse numbers in the index
correspond to those in the Revised Standard
Version of the Bible.*